Annette Wolter

Parakeets

How to Take Care of Them and Understand Them

With 37 color photographs

Drawings by Karin Heckel

Consulting Editor: Matthew M. Vriends, Ph. D.

BARRON'S

Contents

Preface

Being included means everything to a parakeet. Sitting on a human shoulder, being gently scratched, and conversing with "its" person—this is what life can be like, if the owners have enough time to devote to their bird. If you don't have much time, you should buy two parakeets. Life with a parakeet is never dull. And the entertainment will last for at least 12 years, for parakeets that are kept properly can live that long.

What is required to keep these birds happy and healthy is explained in this new pet owner's guide by the parakeet expert Annette Wolter. She tells you in simple terms what to watch for when buying a bird, what its cage should be like and how it should be set up, how to feed a parakeet properly, and what to do if it should get sick. Ms. Wolter also includes concrete advice on how to make your bird friendly and tame, as well as a short course that has helped many parakeet owners teach their birds to talk. All the instructions are precise and easy to follow, so that children, too, can learn how to understand and take proper care of a parakeet.

Lovely color photos by photographers who know parakeets well and keep them themselves convey a vivid picture of this small Australian member of the parrot family that has delighted adults and children all over the world for generations.

The author of the book and the editors of Barron's Series of Pet Owner's Manuals wish you much enjoyment from your parakeet.

Having company is everything to a parakeet. If kept singly, this small parrot pines away unless there is a human being around who is willing to devote himself or herself fully to the bird and play the role of surrogate partner. Anyone who has only limited time should get two parakeets.

Please read the "Important Note" on page 63.

Consider Before You Buy

If your dream is to have a parakeet that will become a friendly member of the family and a cheerful friend, remember that this intelligent small bird also has some desires and requirements for its life with you. It wants affection, human company, freedom to fly, branches for climbing around on, things to nibble on, toys to toss to the floor, someone to pick them up again, and so on. To make sure there won't be any problems later, here are a few points to consider:

Ten Questions to Help You Decide

1. A parakeet can live 12 to 14 years. Are you prepared to assume responsibility for it that long?

2. Do you have a permanent place for the cage?

3. How will you react if your parakeet remains shy and timid and refuses to speak?

4. Do you have enough time to devote to a parakeet?

5. Who will play with the parakeet and whistle tunes to it? Without this kind of attention the bird will languish.

6. What will happen to it when you go away on vacation or if you should have to go to the hospital?

7. Are there other pets in the household that might not get along with the bird? A dog can be taught not to touch the bird, but cats don't respond to such training.

8. Are you planning to give the parakeet to your child as a present? If so, it will still be up to you to watch out for the bird.

9. Are you sure that no one in your family is allergic to bird feathers?

10. Remember that having a bird costs some money, especially if the services of a veterinarian are needed at some point.

Male or Female?

It doesn't matter whether you pick a male or a female. But with a young bird only an expert can tell with any certainty what sex it is. With adult parakeets the male can usually be recognized because its cere, a soft, waxlike covering on the base of the upper mandible, is blue. All females have beige to brownish ceres. In some special color varieties, however, this sure way of telling the sexes apart doesn't work because the male, too, has a beige cere. But if a bird is young, healthy, and lively, its sex is of little consequence.

It is not true that only males can be tamed and may learn to speak. I know many female parakeets that chatter away amusingly and are very friendly.

It is true, however, that females have a greater need to nibble and gnaw, for in nature it is the female who works away at a hole in a tree with her bill until the entry hole and the nesting cavity are just right.

A parakeet is not only beautiful to look at but also abounds with energy, joy at being alive, and affection. If you provide optimal living conditions for the bird, these qualities can come to full expression.

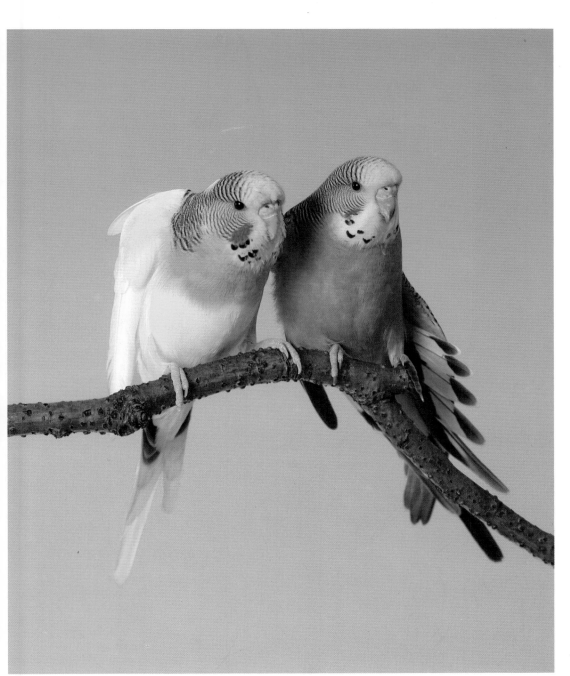

Stretching for comfort is more fun if done in company.

One Bird or a Pair?

Most people want only one parakeet and hope that their bird will be tame, friendly, and playful, take a lively interest in its owner's life, perhaps learn to talk, and be cheerful and happy. Few people realize or give any thought to how much time has to be spent with a bird for it to become this trusting and not to succumb to boredom and apathy. Parakeets are by nature gregarious birds. They are dependent on the community of their flock and especially on the company of their lifelong mate. A parakeet kept as a pet will be happy only if it can develop a strong bond to a human who serves as a surrogate partner. For such a relationship to develop it is necessary, however, not only that this human partner be around the bird almost constantly but also that he or she actively play with the bird, talk to it, whistle tunes to it, and be physically affectionate toward it. Even if such a happy relationship does develop it seems to me that a parakeet that is kept singly is not a real parakeet. For it can never satisfy its inborn need to live the life of one among many in a flock; it will never be able to go through the instinctive ritual that precedes the formation of a lifelong bond with its chosen mate of the same species. You should take full cognizance of this before you buy a single bird. Anyone who is away from home a lot because of work or family obligations would be wiser to get a pair of parakeets not just because they are less time-consuming but also, and above all, because the birds will be happier. It doesn't matter if the two birds are of the same sex because one of them will in time assume the role of the missing gender. You will in any case have the pleasure of watching the elaborate rituals of two parakeets linked by a permanent pair bond. It is even more exciting, of course, if you have a true pair that may actually mate. Such a pair may produce offspring, a subject covered in a separate chapter (see page 47).

Affectionate touching and rubbing of bills is the first step toward lifelong marriage or friendship. Put into words, it means something like "I'm here; please stay with me."

The Colors of the Plumage

The Australian ancestors of our domestically bred parakeets are all light green with a yellow face and forehead. This yellow area, which extends downward to the breast, where there are six black dots, is called the mask. There are also some violet-blue feathers on the sides of the face forming the cheek patches, which are still present in many of the cultivated strains. The back of the head, nape, back, and wing coverts are covered with wavy lines made up of feathers with black and yellow edges. The bill is beige, the cere blue in males and beige to brownish in females.

Birds bred in captivity only rarely preserve the wild coloring; colors like olive green, dark green, sky blue, dark blue, violet, gray, yellow, white, and combinations like clearwings or greywings predominate. Breeders have come up with special names for certain markings. Thus, birds in whom the color of the face mask extends over the head and upper back, forming a V between the markings of the wings, are called "opalines." "Lutinos" are pure yellow with black or red eyes, and "albinos" are white with red eyes. There are also special creations such as the "round crest" with a head reminiscent of the Beatles' hair-dos, and the "feather duster." To me these are a travesty of nature.

My tip: The strains that have the least in common with the original wild parakeet are the most likely to succumb to sickness. Perhaps this hint will help you choose the right kind of bird.

The Right Place for the Cage

For a pet parakeet its cage is its refuge, the place where it feels safe. The cage is its territory and private space, where even the most familiar human should not intrude unnecessarily. In its cage the bird can rest, recover from any fright it may have sustained, eat in peace, and sleep. To serve as such a secure home base, the cage should have a permanent place.

The best place: The living room is the best location, for there the parakeet gets a chance to see the whole family most often. Place the cage in a corner if possible, and near a window, on a shelf that is attached securely to the wall. The shelf should be at a height from which the bird can look at the faces of the people in the room. Parakeets are happiest if they can watch their humans' faces. There should be nothing above the cage because parakeets get scared by activity over their heads.

Very important: The location of the cage should be absolutely free from drafts because drafts make parakeets sick. Check for drafts with a lit candle. Even a draft too slight for us to notice will set the flame flickering.

Raising both wings simultaneously can mean "I'm glad you're back" in parakeet language. Or it can be a way to cool down the body.

Inappropriate locations

• Directly in front of a window: It's too cold in the winter and too hot in the summer.

• The kitchen: Too many dangers—harmful vapors, hot burners, pots and pans with liquid or hot contents, cleansers and other chemicals that are toxic for the bird. Also, it's too drafty when the kitchen has to be aired.

• A child's room: Life here is too boring because children spend most of the day in school, playing, doing sports, going to the movies, and doing home-work. And then they have to go to sleep.

Popular color varieties of parakeets. The original coloration of parakeets is light green with a yellow mask and wavy black-and-yellow "shell" markings on the back of the head, the upper back, and the wing coverts. All the other colors are the result of selective breeding.

Tips For Buying a Bird

Where You Can Buy Parakeets

Pet stores sell parakeets in many colors. You can also buy everything you need to outfit the cage there.

Breeders, too, have parakeets for sale. Get addresses from bird breeders' clubs (see Addresses and Literature page 00) perhaps from an animal shelter or from your local veterinarian.

My tip: Take plenty of time to observe the parakeets offered for sale. Perhaps one of them will appeal to you more than the others because it is so active and playful, or because it looks at you with curious eyes, or because you like its colors, or for some other reason. If you spontaneously find the parakeet that is right for you, the bird's gender is immaterial, for your feelings have spoken, and that is a good way to choose.

Things That Matter

Age of the bird at purchase: The parakeet you buy should be young, about five weeks old, for at this age it will get used to people and a new environment quickly. It should also be healthy so that you can enjoy it for a long time and it will be a good learner.

How to recognize a young parakeet
• It has big, black button eyes, in which the white iris is not yet visible.
• The wavy barring still extends over the entire head, all the way down to the cere, which doesn't turn blue in males until after the prenuptial molt.

What a healthy parakeet looks like
• All the feathers are fully formed; they are lustrous and lie smooth against the body.
• The feathers around the vent—that is what the anal opening of a bird is

For many parakeets, a little bell is an indispensible toy that helps pass the time on the occasions when they have to be left alone.

called—are not sticky or dirty with fecal matter.
• There is no discharge from the eye and nostrils, nor are they encrusted with old, dried-up secretions.
• The horny scales on the feet and toes form a smooth surface.
• On each foot there are two toes pointing forward and two pointing backward. There should be no toe missing.
• The bird moves quickly, grooms itself frequently, and has active contact with its fellows.

A sick parakeet sits apathetically in a corner, its plumage ruffled and its eyes half shut, the bill tucked into the back feathers. If you see a bird like this, take a second look a little while later; perhaps it was just napping.

The Parakeet Cage

Keep in mind when you buy the cage that the future home of your parakeet should not be a prison but a safe refuge and a place for eating and sleeping. The cage should be large enough so that the bird can spread out its wings and at least go through the motions of using them. For even if you are determined to keep your parakeet with the cage door open most of the time, the bird will still, for its own good, have to spend many hours in the closed cage (as when you air the room, clean, have family gatherings).

My tip: Buy your parakeet's cage early enough so that it will be completely set up and ready for occupation on the bird's arrival.

Stands for hanging bird cages are sold by pet supply stores in various designs. They are usually made of metal, are heavy at the bottom, and have a hook at the top from which the cage is hung. This kind of stand makes it is easier to move the cage when that seems desirable.

Warning: Because the heavy foot is usually attached to the top part with a screw, the screw can work itself loose, thus endangering the stand's stability. Check the connection periodically and tighten the screw if necessary. It also happens occasionally that the cage bottom suddenly drops away from the wire part of the cage because the clamps connecting top and bottom were not gripping solidly enough and let go. To forestall such an accident, use a wide rubber band to hold the cage together.

Depending on its mood a parakeet regards its reflection in the mirror as either a partner or a rival. This imagined companion can provide consolation during lonely hours.

What the cage should look like

Ideal dimensions: 40 inches long, 20 inches wide, 32 inches high (100 x 50 x 80 cm).

Minimum dimensions: 20 x 12 x 18 inches (50 x 30 x 45 cm).

Bars: Horizontal on the long sides so that the bird can climb up on them.

Perches: Made of wood and of different thicknesses (1/2 and 3/4 inches, or 12 and 20 mm). The toes should not reach all the way around the perches.

Bottom pan: Made of plastic.

Sand drawer: Should slide in and out.

Food dishes: Two—one for grain, the other for water.

Swing: Usually included in the cage.

My tip: Replace the perches that come with the cage with natural branches of various thicknesses (diameters as given above). For kinds of wood to choose, see A Bird Tree, pages 20 to 22. These branches are not only wonderful to climb around on but also provide work for the bird's bill.

A cage with the minimum dimensions can be used only as a place for the bird to eat and sleep in. For living, a parakeet with such a small cage needs a play area, namely a bird tree.

The so-called indoor aviaries sold by pet supply firms are useful for a pair of birds that you hope to breed, but they are not large enough to serve as flight areas. For that, parakeets need much more space.

My tip: No matter how large its cage, a parakeet still needs a daily session of flying free (see page 19).

The Band

When you buy a parakeet, it often wears a band on its leg that guarantees that it comes from a breeder belonging to a recognized bird society. You should check the banded leg frequently because the bands give rise to many problems. If the band gets caught on something, for instance, the bird will try

Male or female? If you are getting a single bird, the sex makes no difference. Males and females both become friendly and can learn to talk. It is crucial, however, that a person who takes on the role of surrogate partner for a single bird lavish lots of affection on this avian friend.

Parakeets are agile . . .

and fast flyers.

• Mixed birdseed, preferably the kind the parakeet is used to.

• A spray of millet. Millet sprays are a favorite treat and are also highly nutritious (see Things to Enrich the Diet page 38).

• A stone for sharpening the bill. When you buy one, look for a note on the package saying something like "Mineral stone containing all elements necessary for healthy bones and for the formation of feathers."

• A bath house. This is hung in the opened cage door and should have a textured floor so that the bird won't slip when taking a bath.

• Charcoal. If being transported and having to adjust to a new environment has caused diarrhea in the bird, you should sprinkle a little charcoal over the birdseed.

• One or two extra food dishes to be hung on the cage bars for fruit, vegetables, and sprouted seeds.

• Some kind of automatic water dispenser. Water supplied in a water bottle hung upside down in the cage will not get dirty the way it does in a dish.

• Toys, such as a small mirror or a little bell that is hung in the cage. These toys provide some distraction and consolation after the parakeet's separation from its fellows.

• Bird sand for the floor of the cage. The sand not only serves a sanitary function but also contributes to the bird's health (see page 31).

to yank its leg free and may injure itself. If the leg then swells up, the band hinders the blood flow. In such a case the band should be removed by an experienced parakeet breeder or your avian veterinarian. Keep it in a safe place because it represents an important document with which you can prove at any point where your bird came from.

Other Things Your Bird Needs

Before you set out to get your parakeet at the pet store or at the breeder's, make a list of all the things you still would like to get for your bird.

12

A structure of multiple perches is a tempting landing site. Wooden swings like the one shown on this page are available at pet stores. Parakeets like to alight and rest on them after extensive flying in the room.

What a lot of rocking and din a landing can cause!

Gentle Acclimation

The New Home

The new member of the household needs time to adjust to its new and strange surroundings. Don't get impatient if your parakeet takes weeks to shed its shyness and respond to your overtures of friendship.

Bring your parakeet, packed in its little box, home as quickly as possible, protecting it, of course, from cold, dampness, and excessive heat. You want the bird to get used to its new home and quickly get over the sadness of being separated from its siblings. You hope that it will soon overcome its fear of the new, unfamiliar surroundings and come to regard the people with whom it is now living as surrogate partners. At the beginning at least, the cage will be the bird's immediate home and refuge. If possible, you should have it all set up before you go out to buy your bird so that no major last-minute changes will have to be made. Final touches can be added at the very last just before you release your parakeet from its transport box.

The perches inside the cage and on the bird tree have to be thick enough so that the bird's toes don't reach all the way around.

How to Arrange the Inside of the Cage

• Remove the plastic perches. It is best to replace them with natural branches cut to the right length. Either stick them between the bars or tie them in place with string made of raffia.

• Don't put in more branches than there were perches.

• Three branches should be placed horizontally, and one or two at an angle. The branches birds perch on in nature are not all horizontal either.

• Spread bird sand about 1/2 inch (1 cm) deep in the tray at the bottom of the cage.

• Fill one dish with some mixed birdseed, pour water in another, and put pieces of peeled apple and some grated carrot in a third.

• Fasten a spray of millet to the cage bars near one of the branches, using a clothespin or a special clip (available at pet stores).

• Hang the bell from one of the higher branches, and fasten the mirror to the cage in such a way that the bird can see itself when sitting on one of the branches.

My tip: Keep raffia on hand because birds gnaw on it, and it has to be replaced from time to time

The First Few Hours at Home

When you hold the opened transport box against the open cage door, your parakeet is almost certain to emerge from the darkness of the box and move toward the light.

Important: Close the cage door as soon as the bird is inside and move away.

For the next few hours you should refrain from reaching into the cage. Give your parakeet time to examine its new surroundings in peace from the preferably somewhat elevated position of its cage. But stay in the same room and talk to the bird. Say the name you have chosen for it frequently. You will soon notice that the parakeet begins to react to the name, perhaps responding with a sound or with a movement. If it eats a few seeds or pecks at some of the fresh food, this is a sign that the worst shock is over.

The Importance of Night Rest
Time for the parakeet to sleep:
Bedtime comes when you dim the light in the evening and turn the sound of the TV down. Television will not bother the bird if the screen is not directly in its line of vision; if there is any question in your mind, you can drape a light cloth over the cage. The parakeet may still tweet for a while, but gradually it will get drowsy and fall asleep. Leave a small light on for the first few nights, for if the bird is startled by an unfamiliar noise, it may panic and start flapping wildly. Once it realizes it is in its usual surroundings, it is likely to calm down again.

A permanent sleeping place:
Once it has gotten used to its new life, the parakeet will choose a specific, permanent spot for sleeping. It might perch on the swing, favor a certain corner of the cage, or cling to the cage bars near the bell. If the bird has developed such a habit, you have to make sure your parakeet has settled down in its sleeping place before you turn out the lights. If it is in the wrong place, the bird will not sleep well.

Developing Trust
Fear can be a paralyzing, all-consuming feeling. And for as small a creature as a parakeet there are plenty of things to inspire fear and terror. That is why you should be especially careful during the first few weeks to shield your new parakeet from getting frightened. For the more pleasant its first experiences are and the more self-confidence the bird gains in its new environment, the better it will weather later, often unavoidable frights.

How your parakeet will learn to trust you
• Speak to the bird soothingly whenever you have to reach into the cage in the course of the daily cleaning. Say its name a lot, praise it, or sing to it, always the same song. Your voice and tone of voice will have a reassuring effect.

The craving for spray millet makes many a parakeet forget its fear of the human hand. Once the bird feels for a toehold on your finger, you've almost won the game.

• Don't be startled if the bird pecks at your hand; it won't have developed enough courage yet to bite hard.
• Avoid abrupt, hasty movements.
• Try to do the routine cleaning chores at the same time every day.

What is upsetting to your parakeet
Parakeets are creatures of habit and suspicious of anything that looks different. This dislike of change extends to all objects inside the cage as well as to things in the immediate and wider surroundings, and it includes your external appearance. So don't suddenly put a food dish in a different spot, introduce a new toy, or come up to the cage wearing curlers, a black hat, or some other unusual and conspicuous item of clothing. Parakeets also initially

A large cage is a safe haven for one or several parakeets.

regard the human hand as a dangerous or even life-threatening object. They get used to it only gradually and if it is not associated with any frightening experiences. It is therefore important to avoid reaching for a bird that is still shy; all birds are terrified if grasped. Only a bird that is tame and has learned to trust you may be picked up in an emergency.

How birds get used to new things

A bird has to be introduced very gradually to anything new, no matter how small and insignificant it may seem. You have to offer a certain fruit or vegetable it has not had before every day for quite a while before it dares taste it.

A new lamp, for instance, first has to be set up quite far away from the cage and moved just a little bit closer every day before the parakeet accepts it as part of its surroundings. Any unaccustomed or frightening activities or loud noises, such as blowing your nose or vacuuming should at first always be accompanied by the same soothing words. Thus I used to warn Manky, a real "scaredy-cat" of a parakeet, every time before I did it: "Excuse me, but I have to blow my nose." Soon all I had to do was to take out a handkerchief, and Manky would promply comment by saying the same sentence.

Hand-Taming a Parakeet

Once your parakeet has adjusted to its new home, has lost some of the fear of the first days, and has become a little more trusting through daily interaction with you, you can start to get it used to your hand.

The first step: Stop sticking spray millet between the bars and offer it instead from your hand inside the cage every day at the same time. At first the bird will probably not dare get close enough to your hand to peck at the millet but will only eye it briefly and then look away. Remain motionless and talk softly to the bird.

The second step: Perhaps as early as on the second day your parakeet will try from as far away as possible and craning its neck full length to peck a few grains off the millet spray. Or your efforts may go unrewarded for days on end. At some point, however, the parakeet will muster enough courage to try its luck. Just keep offering the millet every day with the same patience and calmness. Soon your hand will look as familiar to your parakeet as the millet spray, and one day the bird will get up on your finger to reach better, though resting on one foot only; the other one is kept on the perch just to be on the safe side.

The third step: Don't lose patience. Eventually the bird will accept your entire hand to perch on, and not just for eating. Soon it will also hop onto your hand to be taken out of the cage and put back in.

My tip: Always offer the back of your hand for the bird to perch on. Many birds are afraid of an open hand.

Avoid at all cost: Never grab a bird except in a great emergency, and never

A parakeet can be hand-tamed with great patience and the use of spray millet.

Dunking the belly in water.

try to catch it in flight! There is no worse terror for a bird than being grasped. Such an experience could ruin the trust in the human hand the bird has developed (see What Is Upsetting To Your Parakeet, page 15).

Getting Used to Baths

If one day you find your parakeet dancing around the waterer and pecking at it, or if it is trying to dip its abdomen into the water dish, this is a clear sign that the bird would like to bathe. At this point you can fill the bath house with

17

about 3/4 inches (2 cm) of lukewarm water and hang it into the cage door opening. If the desire for a bath outweighs the distrust of the unfamiliar bath house, the bird will immediately perch on the tub's edge and start out by taking a few sips of the water.

A full bath: After tasting the water, the bird will step into the water, trembling slightly, lower its abdomen into it, and try to dunk first one spread wing, then the other. Unfortunately the bath house is too small for this. Later, when it has become quite tame, you can offer your parakeet a large flowerpot saucer for bathing, where it can dip at least one wing at a time into the water. But for the beginning a bath house will do.

A dew bath: If your bird doesn't dare approach the bath house even though it has expressed a desire for bathing, hang the bath house in the cage every day from now on, so that the bird can get used to it. You can also rinse some parsley, young dandelion greens, chickweed, or spinach in water and place them, with some of the moisture still on, in the bath house. Many parakeets prefer this kind of "dew bath." After all, they are birds that live on the steppes in nature, where they bathe in the dewy grass while foraging for food in the morning.

My tip: Don't use loose-leaf lettuce for these dew baths because this produce is sprayed against insect pests and to keep it from wilting. The chemicals dissolve in the water and can prove harmful to the bird.

A shower bath: If your parakeet doesn't overcome its distrust of the bath house, you can try giving it showers with a plant mister. The bird doesn't need to be sprayed until it is dripping wet; it merely has to have a chance to get some moisture on its feathers. If it enjoys this "shower," it will turn around in the spray, exposing all parts of the body to the fine mist. If, on the other hand, it acts frightened and tries to get

away, wait until it once more exhibits a desire for bathing and then offer the bath house or a shower again. Don't give up after a few tries; remember that it takes parakeets time to get used to new experiences.

Important: Make sure the spray bottle you are using for the shower has never had plant sprays in it.

It takes time for a parakeet to get used to a bath house. Keep hanging it in the opening of the cage door with some water or wet herbs in the bottom.

A big flowerpot saucer is spacious enough to allow a parakeet to submerge its wings in the water. The bird will probably soon prefer it to a bath house.

Life With a Parakeet

During the period when your parakeet is getting acclimated please don't get the impression that from now on you will have to behave as though you were walking on eggs when you are home. This kind of caution is necessary only during the first few days, or perhaps for the first two to three weeks, depending on your bird's temperament. Even during this initial phase you will experience many happy moments of success. One morning your parakeet will show its pleasure at seeing you and shake its plumage vigorously. It will start to respond to your greetings or whistled tunes by tweeting back cheerfully, or it may display its trusting mood by setting the bell ringing while you are still cleaning the cage. These are all indications that your parakeet is getting more and more interested in its new world and would like to explore a wider territory. The best way to satisfy this desire is to let the bird fly free in the room. But to make sure that your bird won't encounter any mishaps and can enjoy free flying without constant supervision, I would like to recommend a few useful procedures based on my own experience.

Flying Without Risks

A parakeet gets to know its new environment best and most quickly if it can fly around in it often and for extended periods of time. This not only helps a bird feel comfortable in its new surroundings but is also good for its health. But before you open the cage, close all doors and windows in the room and draw the window curtains. Since birds don't recognize glass as a barrier, your parakeet might crash against a window with full force and injure or even kill itself. One way to get a parakeet used to curtainless windows is to lower shades all but about 8 inches (20 cm), turning on the light if it gets too dark in the room. Then increase the uncovered part of the windows a little bit every day until the bird has learned to regard windows as a barrier. Usually this takes only a few days.

A parakeet is so flexible that it can reach all parts of the body with its bill when preening its plumage.

The First Flight

If at first your parakeet just sits there, staring through the open cage door as though hypnotized, and doesn't immediately launch itself into the free air, don't worry. Remember that it probably has never before had a chance to fly. In the nest box there wasn't enough room, and in the communal cage it probably couldn't do much more than flutter its wings.

Some parakeets become so tame and friendly that they like to perch on the shoulder of "their" human for hours and watch with interest whatever the person does. They are especially happy if the person keeps "chatting" with them.

19

Parakeet games: Pulling on a doily . . .

pecking at some seeds in a glass . . .

Give the bird plenty of time: At some point it won't be able to resist the temptation to take a closer look at the room it sees beyond the open rectangle. Perhaps it will first climb on top of the cage. But soon the urge to fly will overcome fear, and your parakeet will take to its wings and cross the room for the first time.

Landing maneuvers: Flying itself presents no problems, but landing may be a different story—first of all because your bird probably has never done it before, and secondly because there are so many unfamiliar, fear-inspiring things in the room. With some luck the bird may be able to alight on the cage. If that is the case, leave it up to your parakeet whether it wants to have another go at it or whether it prefers to retreat to the safety of the cage. The next day it will go about flying with much less hesitation.

How to lure the bird back into the cage: If your parakeet lands on the floor, put down some birdseed for it. Parakeets love to forage for food on the ground. Then, when you place the cage near it a little bit later, the bird will probably be happy to climb back in. Should your bird land on a bookcase, a

lamp, or a curtain rod, the return flight becomes a test of courage. The higher the spot where it has landed, the safer the bird feels. This feeling is instinctive because in nature a high perch usually means greater safety from predators. And now it is supposed to abandon this place of refuge? Overcoming the reluctance is a major struggle and takes time. Talk to the bird, and try to lure it off its perch with a spray of millet. If your efforts are futile, hold the open cage up to the bird after about half an hour. Perhaps it will step into it, relieved. If not, leave the bird sitting where it is. It will manage a safe return eventually, even if not until the next morning.

Avoid at all cost: Don't even consider chasing the bird or trying to dislodge it by waving a piece of cloth at it. This sort of thing would destroy all the trust the bird has developed.

A Bird Tree

Once my first parakeet discovered how much more fun it was to sit outside the cage rather than in it, it took to spending almost the entire day outside the cage. It would fly through the room now and then, but always landed on the cage, from where it watched me work at *and setting the bell ringing.*

my desk. Whenever I left it alone, it would seek refuge on the indoor linden (*Sparmannia africana*). But the plant's branches were much too thin to make good perches, so I attached some natural branches to the tree for the bird to sit on. Now the linden tree became the parakeet's favorite spot. But when, soon after, a second parakeet joined our household, the plant did not survive for long. The two parakeets loved to nip off branches and let the leaves sail down to the floor. At this point I decided to buy a large tub of the kind used for hydroculture and built my first bird tree. This artificial tree became—and for many years remained—a haven of delight for my birds in the middle of my study.

Of course the branches of such a tree and the raffia strings tying them together have to be replaced every few months, but when I watched the delight with which my birds nibbled on the branches, the time and effort spent seemed well worth while. You do, however, have to be careful about what branches to pick.

Use only nonpoisonous branches

Fruit tree branches are ideal, but only if you are absolutely sure that they haven't been sprayed. If you have the slightest doubt, it is better to pick branches from other trees, such as oak, alder, elderberry, chestnut, basswood, poplar, or willow. Even here you have to be careful: Don't gather them near roads and highways because everything there is contaminated with chemicals from car emissions. These poisonous substances are absorbed by the wood. Even branches from parks and from the woods should be hosed off with hot water and let dry before a bird touches them, for even parks are not safe from harmful substances, and acid rain falls everywhere.

How to Construct a Bird Tree

• Put a few heavy stones in the bottom of a large flower pot or tub to lend stability.

• In the middle of this pot place a smaller flower pot with a *nonpoisonous* vine

• Use wire to attach three or four branches or bamboo sticks about 6 feet (2 m) long and 1 1/4 inches (3 cm) thick vertically to the smaller pot.

• Fill the space between the smaller pot and the edge of the larger one with earth and top with bird sand.

• Now connect the vertical branches

In the photos:
Many things make good toys. Even simple objects in your apartment can offer amusement to a parakeet. Just watch out that the bird doesn't start nibbling on something that could be harmful.

21

Incorporating a living plant in the bird tree is especially ideal if you have two parakeets that are still getting acquainted. The plant provides cover so that the birds can hide from each other until they decide to make friends.

with natural branches 1/2 to 3/4 inches (12–20 mm) thick to form several "floors," tying the horizontal branches to the vertical sticks with raffia string. Not all these connecting branches have to be absolutely horizontal; after all, the bird is supposed to do a lot of climbing in the tree.

Pet birds need a place where they can spend time comfortably outside their cage. A bird tree with natural branches can become a beloved mini-environment for birds.

• Tie a little bell and a mirror to different branches in such a way that they are at eye level with the bird when it sits on a branch. The best place is near a forked branch, for parakeets like to perch on forked branches.

• Replace the branches and the string, as well as the branches in the cage, every few weeks.

My tip: Check to see that the perching branches don't stick out beyond the rim of the larger tub. If they do, some of the droppings will land on the floor instead of in the bird sand.

Where to Put the Tree

Needless to say, the bird tree needs a permanent spot in the room. It is best if it is placed at some distance from the cage, because then the bird is forced to fly back and forth several times a day. While a parakeet is young and full of energy, it needs no special urging to fly, but as it gets older and perhaps a little lazier, having to fly to and from the tree is a good counterbalance to a sedentary way of life. It should also go without saying that food and water are offered in the cage only; otherwise the bird may be tempted not to bother flying back at all. A good place for the bird tree is next to a window. There the parakeet can watch birds flying outside and there is plenty of light during the day.

A Bird-proof Room

Probably no birdkeeper, no matter how conscientious, will succeed in eliminating all sources of danger that lurk in a room inhabited by both birds and humans. I have all too often seen these small, agile avian creatures discover fascinating things we humans are quite oblivious of. Thus one time when she was getting ready to brood, my female parakeet Clowny tried successfully to squeeze through a space about 1 1/4 inches (3 cm) wide between the ceiling and a bowl-shaped glass ceiling lamp. The lamp was smooth on the outside, but on the inside the glass had veins with knife-sharp edges. By the time we had freed her, her feet were bloody. Nevertheless she renewed her efforts to nest there until we stuffed the space between ceiling and lamp with rags. Another incident spurred me on to renew my vigilance in bird-proofing the room. When I came home one day, I found all the birds but one in their favorite places. Only the youngest, Sibyll, was nowhere to be seen. I couldn't imagine where she might be and looked in all conceivable hiding places—in vain. Then a soft rustling in

Dangers Lurking for Your Parakeet

Dangers	How to avoid the danger:
Bathroom: Escape through a casement window; drowning in the toilet.	Keep bathroom door closed. Let bird in only when you are present.
Bookshelves: Bird hides behind books and can't get out again without help.	Push books flush against the wall or lay a couple of books flat at intervals.
Floor: If the bird plays on the floor it can be stepped on and killed.	Get in the habit of being extremely careful wherever you step.
Containers with water: The bird slips into a bucket, bowl, large glass, or vase and drowns (soapsuds are often mistaken for a solid landing site).	Cover containers; don't let bird fly free when you clean house.
Closets, open drawers: The bird is licked in inadvertently and suffocates or starves to death.	Never leave them open even a crack.
Poisons: Fatal poisoning can be caused by alcohol, the lead in pencils, the points of magic markers and ballpoint pens, strong spices, verdigris, adhesives, varnishes, glues, solvents, fertilizers, plastic wrap, cleansers, mercury, strong-smelling sprays, laundry detergents, heavy cigarette smoke.	Keep all these substances and objects locked away where the bird can't get at them. Remove all traces of them.
Stovetop burners: Fatal burns if bird lands on a hot burner.	Put pots or kettles with cold water on burners that are still hot. Never let bird fly unsupervised in kitchen.
Burning candles: Fatal burns if bird flies through the flame.	Do without candlelight while the bird flies free.
Wastepaper basket, ornamental vases: Sliding in, starving to death or dying of heart failure if bird feels trapped.	Use woven waste baskets or line the inside with wire mesh. Fill vases with sand.
Direct sun, hot car: Heart failure caused by heat stroke.	Place cage in shade. Air the car.
Stoves, electrical appliances: Death caused by burns.	Locate then where they can't be reached by the bird.
Temperature fluctuations: Abrupt changes lead to colds or cause heat stroke.	Get bird accustomed to different temperatures in the range of 41° to 77°F (5°-25°C).

A t first
parakeets
don't realize that
windows are solid
barriers. To keep
them from
crashing into the
glass, they should
be allowed to fly
in the room only
when curtains are
drawn or shades
lowered. If a little
more of the glass
is exposed every
day, the bird will
gradually get
used to windows.

the waste basket caught my attention. Sibyll had probably slipped off the rim of the basket and, once fallen in, could not get out of this smooth "tube" without help.

The Greatest Danger: Escaping

Six out of ten pet parakeets escape at some point. That is a a disheartening statistic, if you keep in mind that in the climatic conditions of various parts of the country the birds have no chance of survival. To make things worse, parakeets are unable to make use of striking landmarks to help them orient themselves. It is an ability they have no need for in their original nomadic life in Australia. That is why a lost parakeet never finds its way back home and will die unless it happens to be found and taken in by someone. For these reasons the first and foremost rule for any parakeet owner is to keep doors and windows closed at all times. A parakeet can escape even from a closed cage by squeezing through the crack of the drawer opening if the sand tray is left out for a moment, or it may learn to open the cage door with its strong bill. Curtains in front of an open window offer no protection against escape either because the bird may climb up on them, wend its way snakelike through the narrow space between two curtain rings, and take off. That is why at least one window in the bird room should have a strong metal screen with spaces between the wires no larger than 3/8 by 3/8 inches (1 x 1 cm). The screen should be mounted on a wooden frame that fits tightly into the window opening. This way you won't have to worry about airing the room, and you can let the bird live in it without constant supervision.

Plants in the Bird Room

The plants to be kept in the bird room either for decoration or as a supplement to the bird tree also have to be chosen with care for they can be a source of

danger as well. Here is a list of ones to watch out for:

Poisonous indoor plants: The bird should never be in contact with any of the following: poison primrose (*Primula obconica*), *Strychnos nux-vomica,* Amaryllis, (*Amaryllis* species), crown-of-thorns, all dieffenbachia species, yew, hyacinth, azalea, boxwood, periwinkle (*Vinca minor*), all nightshades, such as coral plant *Jatropha multifida*; also, narcissus, oleander, yam bean berries of ardisia plants, poinsettia, variegated laurel (*Codiaeum variegatum*), mistletoe, the berries of ornamental asparagus, and datura.

The following plants are not poisonous but do contain substances that irritate the mucous membrane and can be quite harmful to such small creatures as birds: ivy, monstera, flamingo flower, Chinese evergreen, *Aglaonema*, philodendron, and schefflera.

Be especially careful with cacti of all kinds and other plants with thorny or prickly parts; the birds can hurt their eyes on them.

Important: When you buy new plants, ask about their compatibility with birds. New kinds of plants, not included in our list, are becoming available all the time.

Nonpoisonous house plants: These can, of course, be enjoyed by you and your bird. But it is always possible that your parakeet will take a special liking to one or another of them and prune it lovingly with its beak until there is not much left of it.

Boredom Is Harmful

Anyone who has a pet parakeet should keep in mind that a bird simply can't live the kind of life it was meant to live in an apartment designed for human occupancy. Even a pair of birds don't have enough to do to keep them busy. They don't spend time and energy in the search for food, they are rarely if ever absorbed in parental duties, the female

This parakeet is settling down in a relaxed mood on a hand it knows well.

doesn't have to claim and prepare a nest cavity, the male doesn't have to defend the nest site against rivals, and the birds don't even have to worry about predators. To be sure, wild birds are not active every moment from dawn to dusk and take short naps several times during the day, and the intensive grooming of the plumage takes up time; still, if there is no other incentive to play and work with the bill, even young parakeets quickly become bored. These spirited, highly energetic, and intelligent birds have to be able to play, and they need encouragement and inspiration from their human partners to put their talents to good use.

Popular Toys

For a parakeet, having a partner of its own species around is the ideal way to dispel boredom. But even two birds can't keep on reestablishing their hierarchical positions indefinitely; and they are not always in a courtship mood. Parakeets spend a surprising amount of time picking away at fresh branches and playing with objects. These objects don't always necessarily have to be toys. Anything that makes the birds move around and is used by them in different ways is fine. In pet stores you will find the following toys for parakeets:

Small bells. Birds like these especially because they are made of shiny metal in which the birds can see themselves.

Mirrors that can be hung in the cage or are mounted on a weighted toy that always comes to rest with the mirror on top. Usually parakeets spend a lot of time with such a mirror because they keep jabbing at their reflection, which they take for a rival bird, and then running away to keep from being bumped when the mirror swings back or pops up again. Parakeets catch on quickly to the behavior of the mirror and like spending time with their imaginary foe.

Plastic birds. These can be clamped to a perch, and some parakeets beat up such a plastic companion like a rival, while others try to feed it like a partner or like a hungry baby bird. To a male bird, it represents the missing female partner, and to a female, nestlings.

Solid balls or whiffle balls with or without a bell inside. These are made of plastic. A bird can play properly with such a ball only if you join in the game.

Items a bird finds among your belongings:

Small wooden objects. These may have been bought at the pet store or they may simply be around and appeal to your bird's instinct for play. Quite often, too, a bird will pick an object to serve as a friend and surrogate partner and display passionate love toward it. This may be a thimble, a marble, a tiny metal box, a chess or other boardgame figure, a die, or—as I once observed in the bird clinic in West Germany—even a small shot glass. In this clinic a sick parakeet in an isolation cage was huddling as close as it could get to the glass to find consolation in its misery.

A mirror is an indispensible toy for a parakeet that is kept singly.

From the bird's owner I found out that this glass was very important and provided great comfort to the bird in all kinds of situations.

Important: All toys that are hung must be attached to a short, not too thin chain or a short, heavy string so that the bird cannot strangle itself on the chain or string. The toys also have to be washed from time to time with hot water.

Stimulating Play

To be able to cope with the various challenges and demands of life in the wild, parakeets are equipped with intelligence, physical agility, and excellent flying skills. In the life of a pet bird, all this potential lies idle. A physically and emotionally healthy parakeet transmutes these native talents into curiosity, interest in vocal mimicry, and inventive play. It likes to make use of the toys described above to occupy itself. But if a bird is left to its own devices, its interest and enthusiasm soon flag. It needs you to be able to play properly. It likes to set a ball rolling or it may shove it deliberately toward the edge of a table, and when the ball drops to the floor, it watches with interest. If you pick up the ball and perhaps put it back in the middle of the table, the parakeet will patter up to it enthusiastically to continue the game. A parakeet can pick up a whiffle ball with a bell inside, lift it high with its bill, carry it across the entire table, and toss it at you. If you roll the ball back toward the bird, it will either get out of the way timidly or walk straight up to it to toss it back. If you set a little bell swinging, the bird will run after it, as though playing tag, to give it another shove, and then quickly dodge as it swings back.

For me the whiffle ball became something of an exercise machine. My parakeet Manky would hold the ball in his bill, sitting on the top branch of the bird tree, and toss it at me. But very often I had to bend to pick the ball up off the floor because the smart bird was clever enough to make me miss the ball.

Keeping Busy when Alone

Your parakeet will now keep a sharp eye on you to figure out when you are ready to play again. If it notices no such indication, it will turn to other activities. Grooming or preening its plumage alone takes up considerable time every day. No feather goes untended. With great skill the parakeet pulls each flight feather on the wings and the tail through its bill to free it from dust, smoothe it, and oil it lightly. The same is done with the contour feathers. To oil its plumage the bird rubs its head over the oil gland at the base of the tail or picks up oil and distributes it with its bill. The acrobatic skill displayed in preening is amazing. Except for the head, which birds allow their partners to preen, there is no place on the body that is not reached by the bill.

Ever so often birds need to take short rests. They often assume their sleeping posture, nap or doze a little, and become completely oblivious of their surroundings. Then they wake up again refreshed and ready for new action. They may nibble on branches or on house plants within their reach, or they may go after papers, books, wallpaper, or posters with special gusto. But don't worry too much. These are often just phases. For the first few months I had parakeets, all my manuscripts had jagged edges, but after a while pecking at the papers lost its attraction, and the birds turned to my books. I was more finicky about books and hung sheets over my bookshelves. In time the books, too, lost their fascination, and for a long time the birds' interest focused on my rock collection, where they couldn't do much damage.

Important: Parakeets continually need new incentives to use their beaks. Be sure you always supply them with fresh branches, cuttlebone, and pumice or other stone for sharpening the bill.

Times of Intimate Togetherness

Playing, working with its beak, and resting are not the only things a para-

Raising itself to its full height, this bird has carried the ball across the table. If you are willing to play, a real game can now start.

keet wants to do. The most precious minutes of the day for a bird are when it can perch on your finger or shoulder and listen to your voice. If it hears its name, musical tunes, or short sentences often enough it may try to repeat them. If you begin to detect the first words in its chattering, it is worthwhile patiently encouraging this talent. The bird will listen, entranced, several times a day to all the words it can already pronounce and also to new ones. Perhaps your particular parakeet has more of a gift for whistling or for imitating other sounds. Don't be disappointed if this is the case. Indulge in daily chatting sessions anyway because the bird loves being very close to you.

The best way to get the bird's full and undivided attention is to be in a room that is absolutely quiet when the daylight begins to fade and when there is

nothing to distract the bird. This is also the right moment to try scratching the bird's head very gently. A parakeet has to get used to this gradually because at first it is suspicious of your finger. Try with the tip of your little finger, or with the shaft of a flight feather the bird has shed. Birds like being scratched best on the head and neck because they can't reach these areas with their bill. Once your bird realizes what you are trying to do, it will quickly lose its shyness and enjoy the scratching. In return it will probably start "preening" your eyelashes, eyebrows, and skin very affectionately, nibbling away gently.

A Course for Developing a Bird's Talent for Talking

Parakeets with a talent for talking will repeat many expressions they hear a lot, such as greetings, names, verbal interdictions, swear words, or the "hello" you use to answer the telephone. If you would like to teach your parakeet specific expressions, however, observe the following rules:

• In situations that recur regularly, always say the same, appropriate expression. Say "good morning" when you first enter the room in the morning, "good night" before turning out the light in the evening, or "here's a treat" when you bring food.

• Always say the same short phrase—using the same speaking rhythm—whenever the bird looks at you expectantly.

• Sing or whistle short tunes to the bird several times a day.

• During your moments of closeness,

Spray millet, the favorite food of cage birds. But don't let your parakeets eat their fill of it because they would get a much too one-sided diet.

repeat all the vocabulary the bird has already learned. Be sure to make time for these sessions of intimate togetherness at least once every day.

• Perhaps you can tape the bird's repertoire of phrases and other sounds. Play the tape for it when the bird has to stay by itself for a short time.

Manky, the most gifted talker of all my parakeets, always flopped down on his belly in front of the tape player and listened with rapture. He knew the sequence of everything on the tape by heart and always started the next phrase wherever I had paused for breath when recording.

Using Words Appropriately

One keeps hearing stories about birds that respond to certain situations with appropriate expressions. Usually these birds are African gray parrots. Parakeets are capable of this feat, too. Thus, my parakeet Jackele would often sit next to Clowny, cooing tenderly, and repeat over and over: "Clowny, I love you so much." Of course he had heard me say this, but he only said it to Clowny, never to me or to one of the other parakeets. Or when visitors came and asked Manky "Well, and who are you?" he would answer promptly "Manky Wolter of Planegg." During the summer we often had a visitor spend time with us. This was Maxi, a parakeet that ordinarily lived without the company of other birds. Maxi didn't quite know what to make of our birds, and he liked flying free best when they were locked up. To give vent to their resentment they would move around in their cages with such acrobatic twistings and turnings that I would soon let them out, too. Then, whenever Manky got too close to Maxi, the latter would call out in great agitation "Lock him up, lock him up!" which was what the grandmother in Maxi's family, who was afraid of birds, always said.

G ive your bird a short, simple name that it can repeat easily. Teaching a parakeet to talk takes lots of patience and doesn't always lead to the desired results. This should in no way spoil your enjoyment of your avian pet.

Parakeets Are Intelligent

Professor Otto König, an ethologist working in Vienna, reports that he succeeded in training birds to count. According to him, parakeets, like jackdaws, can count up to six, which they demonstrate by picking up seeds. Pigeons can count up to the number five, while common ravens, yellow-fronted Amazons, and African gray parrots get all the way to seven. In the course of daily interaction with your parakeet, you, too, will notice signs of intelligence in your bird. One example of intelligence is the way a bird will slip out of its cage in a flash as soon as it notices that you are about to close the cage door.

My parakeet Jojo's favorite toy used to be a two-colored whiffle ball with a little bell inside it. I always had several of these balls on hand, but he preferred one particular one and only played with it. If I secretly substituted another, outwardly identical ball, he would refuse to play with it, visibly sad, and look for "his" ball everywhere. If I gave it back to him together with four other balls, he would run up to his favorite ball excitedly and completely ignore the others.

Manky found a clever way to circumvent his species' instinctive inhibition of aggression against females of the species. He had a favorite spot on my desk in front of a small onyx box, where I sometimes gave him his favorite food, hulled oats. He would eat them there ecstatically, lying practically flat on his belly. If, occasionally, he found his mate Mini there eating "his" oats, he resorted to the following trick: With pretended innocence he would try to engage me in playing with him, using one of the above-mentioned whiffle balls, but he would do his best to toss the ball not toward me but at Mini, so that she would be driven away from the oats, a scheme that worked quite often.

When Manky was still my only parakeet he would watch everything I did like a hawk. When I had to go away for a longer time than usual, he must have had some way of telling this from my preparations. He would then sit on his tree with his back to me. When I was finally ready to depart, he would fly at me with a scream and try to hide inside my collar. This made me feel so sorry for him that I soon brought Mini home to keep him company.

Birds bury their bills in their back feathers not only when they sleep at night but also for short rests during the day.

A Second Parakeet

Of course I had my doubts at first about acquiring a second bird. Would Manky continue to be as friendly and affectionate with me when he had the constant company of another parakeet? Would he stop his charming talking? When I first introduced Mini to him I held her in my two hands so that only her head was visible. Manky ran up to her and brutally yanked a feather from her head. Mini screamed, and I immediately took her away. Manky had probably reacted out of jealousy. The next day I set Mini, who was not yet able to fly, down on the floor in front of Manky. He

A parakeet can put a whiffle ball like this to all kinds of uses, but it will be happiest if you join in the game.

looked at her briefly from the desk where he was perched, and he must have recognized how young she was. In any case, he immediately began to feed her and continued to do so until she was completely independent.

His relationship with me didn't change in any way, and Mini was simply included in the friendship. Manky never again reacted jealously to her, but he insisted that our play and chatting periods be continued. Mini's interest, however, was concentrated almost exclusively on the partner of her own species, and she regarded me more as someone to fall back on when needed, a friend one could count on when one found oneself in a tight spot.

Acclimating a second bird

• The sex of the second parakeet is immaterial. If the two birds turn out to be of the same sex, one of them will assume the role of the missing gender. However, the new bird should be of fledgling age so that the older one can respond to it by assuming a parental role.

• If possible, start out by housing the new bird by itself for a week, and spend a lot of time with it. This will help it overcome its timidity and fear of you.

• When you first bring the birds together, leave the cage door open. Then they can get out of each other's way if the older bird doesn't accept the newcomer right away.

Hygiene Is Necessary

Like all pets, parakeets create some dirt. But what they leave behind is easily removed with a vacuum cleaner. It takes a little more time to maintain the hygienic conditions necessary for the bird to thrive. If these chores aren't performed regularly, the bird will get sick. The cage, the bird tree, and all the accessories have to be kept clean. The best way to proceed is to draw up a cleaning schedule.

Schedule of Chores
Daily

• Remove with a spoon the soiled parts of the sand in the cage bottom and in the tub with the bird tree. Top with some fresh sand.

Caution: The bird might escape through the crack when you take out the sand tray. To be on the safe side, plug the open slit with a book or a damp cloth.

• Empty all the dishes, and perhaps the water bottle, wash them out with hot water, dry well, and fill them again. Fill the seed dish about half way.

• Scrub dirty branches with sandpaper and wipe them with a damp cloth.

• Check in the afternoon to see if there is enough birdseed left. If there are too many empty hulls, remove them with a small spoon. Don't try to blow them off the seeds because this raises too much dust.

Weekly

• Wash out and dry the cage bottom and the sand tray. Use warm water.

• Wash the mirror and the bell with hot water and dry them.

• Discard leftover birdseed. Rinse all dishes in hot water, dry, and refill them.

Monthly

• Wash the entire cage down with hot water in the bathtub, scrubbing all parts with a brush. Then rub everything dry, let wooden items dry out some more in the air.

• Replace gnawed branches in the cage and on the bird tree with fresh ones that have been washed in hot water and dried well.

Important: It is better not to use an automatic food dispenser because these feeders clog easily. If not enough seeds slide down, a bird can starve to death in front of a filled feeder. Don't use detergents or cleansers for cleaning. The chemicals in them are toxic to the birds. Clean water about 130°F (55°C) is quite adequate and presents no danger.

A cord hanging from the cage ceiling is used by many parakeets for climbing and other acrobatics. Very trusting birds even let themselves be swung around on it in circles as on a merry-go-round.

A gentle invitation to be scratched . . .

In the photos:
Natural branches for climbing on and nibbling. Parakeets feel most comfortable on these branches. The birds' toes can get a good grip on them, and they provide plenty of opportunity for gnawing (see pages 21–22). Be sure to use only nonpoisonous branches that will not harm your pet (see page 24). Unfortunately even biologists cannot always be relied on to know which plants are poisonous, but from experience I know that all yew, oleander, boxwood, and dieffenbachia species are to be avoided.

which sometimes has to be repeated a little more forcefullly.

What to Do with the Bird during Vacations

If you would like to go away on vacation you have to make plans not just for yourself but also for your bird.

Vacations abroad are out of the question for parakeets because entry regulations applying to members of the parrot family are so stringent.

A trip by car is possible. But if the parakeet comes along you have to make sure there are no drafts in the car even during hot summer weather. If you stay in a hotel or motel, the bird has to stay inside its cage because the cleaning personnel doesn't always keep doors and windows closed. A camp ground is not a good place for a parakeet; but a vacation cottage represents a homelike atmosphere that the bird may be able to enjoy.

Staying at home in its familiar surroundings is by far the best alternative for your parakeet, assuming that a reliable caretaker can be found to look after the bird and talk and play with it twice a day.

Having one's head scratched all over is a wonderful feeling.

Boarding the bird, perhaps with friends or relatives, is another possibility, but give the temporary bird keepers exact instructions on the bird's needs and send along all the things your parakeet needs to be happy. Make sure that the bird will be able to fly free a lot in its temporary lodgings.

Pet stores sometimes board parakeets for a small fee. But a bird will not be able to fly free there.

In case of illness: Should you have to go to the hospital, whether unexpectedly or for some planned treatment, I recommend that you choose one of the last three alternatives mentioned above.

Advice to parrot owners living alone: Look for a reliable per son to look after your bird before the need arises.

My tip: Animal shelters often have names and addresses of bird lovers willing to take in one or two birds for a vacation or in an emergency. Try to contact and get together with such a person before you need him or her, so that arrangements can be made quickly if the need arises.

The Proper Diet

Only viable seeds are rich in the nutrients that keep parakeets healthy. That is why you should look for the date on the package when you buy birdseed. You should also test the seeds' viability whenever you open a new package.

A Parakeet's Diet in the Wild

In their Australian homeland parakeets feed on the seeds of different grasses and other plants. If they pass through arid regions in their continual search for food, they stay near watering places because they need drinking water to soften the dry grains in their crops. If all the streams and pools of water dry up, the birds move around on the ground in their early morning foraging and drink the dew hanging from the blades of grass. It has been shown that they also eat some fresh greens and pick up tiny grains of mineral-rich sand, which is needed for proper digestion. As soon as a rainy period starts, the parakeets get ready to breed because in a few days the grass and herbs will sprout new shoots. These plants will also soon produce half-ripe seeds, a highly nutritious food needed both by breeding parents and baby birds; without these seeds, raising offspring would be out of the question.

Parakeets particularly enjoy picking up seeds from the floor, a habit that goes back to their wild ancestors, who foraged on the ground for all their food.

Seeds as the Basic Staple

Our knowledge of the feeding habits of wild parakeets has made it possible to come up with properly balanced seed mixtures that can serve as the basic staple in our pet parakeets' diet. Such a mixture consists mainly of canary grass seeds and several varieties of millet, to which oats, niger seed, and linseed are added. Good commercial mixtures often contain thistle as well, and pet food companies also add iodine grains to prevent enlargement of the thyroid.

Important: Always look at the packing date when you buy birdseed. It is stamped on the package and should not be dated back more than about 3 months because there is no telling how long the seed was stored before being packaged. All commercially available grains and seeds are harvested once a year and remain viable for one year, though they are edible for two if stored properly. But since the nutritive value gradually declines even if seeds are stored properly, you should test the viablility of each package you open. If the seeds germinate, they are still high in nutritive value (see Directions for Sprouting Seeds, page 39).

If only a small proportion of the seeds sprout, the mixture is useless and should not be fed to the bird.

Signs of deterioration

• Rot: Rotting seeds have a strong odor; healthy seeds don't smell.

• Mildew: You can recognize mildew by the whitish-grayish fuzz on the seeds, but you have to look the seeds over very carefully to detect it.

• Vermin: Seeds that are clumped together and have cobweb-like filaments emanating from them indicate vermin.

Storing seeds properly: If you have only one or two parakeets, a package of birdseed will last you several weeks. While using up a package, you should store the seeds in a dark, dry, and airy place, just like grain for your own consumption.

Correct way: Hang the seeds in an appropriate place in a bag made of natural fiber, or plastic. Or store the seed in the refrigerator.

Incorrect way: Putting the seeds in a paper bag, an open tin, or an open jar.

How Much Birdseed a Day?

• Put 2 teaspoonfuls per bird into the seed cup every morning; if you use 2 cups, put 1 teaspoonful in each.

• Skim the empty husks off the top in the early afternoon because otherwise your bird will not be able to get at the seeds underneath.

• If there are just a few seeds left in the cup in the evening, add half a teaspoonful more so that the bird will find something to eat first thing in the morning, when it needs food for energy.

It is correct to make sure your bird always has sufficient food at its disposal. You might sometimes be delayed on your way home after work, and then a well stocked seed cup is a real blessing.

It is wrong to try to keep a bird from getting fat by rationing the birdseed it gets. Birds have a very active metabolism and need small amounts of food frequently. Birds become overweight only if their diet is wrong, if they don't get enough exercise, or if they don't have enough to keep them busy. So avoid unnecessary, fattening treats, such as the hearts, bars, and so on, sold in pet stores, that are covered with seeds stuck on with sugar or honey.

My tip: Don't blow the empty seed husks out of the cup. This is messy if done inside and dangerous if done at an open window because your bird might escape.

Drinking Water

Of course your parakeet needs fresh water every day. Tap water that is not too cold is fine, but if you want to offer your bird something especially healthy, buy noncarbonated mineral water. The label on the bottle usually lists the health-promoting minerals contained in the water. Only sick birds should get boiled water or, if an avian vet recommends it, weak black tea or camomile tea.

Vegetables and Fruit

If you want your parakeet to stay healthy and live long, keep its beautiful plumage, and not get obese, you should give it plenty of fruits and vegetables that are in season and as fresh as possible. The best way to incorporate fresh produce into the parakeet's diet is to follow your own menu plan and give the bird some of everything that is good for it.

Raw vegetables: Eggplant, a little bit of avocado, endive, green peas, young dandelion greens, corn kernels, fresh corn especially if it is at the "milky" stage, Swiss chard, carrots, unsprayed lettuce, sorrel, spinach, parsley, radish, red beets, alfalfa, celery, zucchini, curly kale, brussels sprouts, sweet potato, and dock.

Fruit: Fresh pineapple, apple, apricot, banana, pear, blackberries, strawberries, cotoneaster berries, elder berries, goose berries, mulberries, fresh figs, dates, rasperries, cherries, kiwi fruit, mango, tangerine, melon, orange, peach, grapes, currants, guava.

Things that don't agree: All kinds of cabbage, raw and green potatoes, green beans, lettuce sprayed with pesticides, grapefruit, rhubarb, plums, lemons.

Important: Feed nothing directly from the refrigerator; all food should be at room temperature and have been washed, rubbed or dabbed dry, and peeled.

A practical holder for spray millet, in which even smallish pieces can be offered.

Cleaning the tail feathers requires the skills of an acrobat.

How to Offer Raw Vegetables and Fruit

Fruits and vegetables that are of solid consistency, like pineapple, apples, avocados, pears, carrots, and zucchini, are cut into slices or sections thick enough to stick between the cage bars. Soft fruits are cut into small pieces, mixed with berries, peas, shredded leafy vegetables, and perhaps some grated vegetables, and offered in a shallow bowl.

Don't be discouraged if your bird doesn't realize immediately what delicacies it is being given. Perhaps it just barely touches the food with its bill. If its taste buds come into contact with the juice of a fruit, the bird may then be brave enough to take a bite. Often it takes days or even weeks before a parakeet develops a liking for fresh food and starts looking forward to it as a treat.

Parakeets that are already used to fresh food sometimes love to just peck and nibble at it. They may bite pieces off a slice of carrot or a piece of apple and leave some of them. The impulse behind this behavior is the pleasure of taking things apart. But minute quantities of the fruit are absorbed and supply necessary vitamins even if most of it is not eaten. When you consider how little a parakeet weighs, you can appreciate that though its body's need for these substances is crucial, it is small compared to ours.

Minerals and Trace Elements

Like people, parakeets need these substances only in minute quantities. Seeds as well as fresh foods contain small amounts. The most important, calcium and phosphorus, are present in the mineral block the bird uses to sharpen its beak on and in the bird sand. When buying a mineral block, always watch for a note on the package saying something like "Calcium block, containing all elements necessary for strengthening the skeleton and forming feathers." Make sure you always have a stone in reserve, for quite often a bird will suddenly go to work avidly on the block in the cage, reducing it to nothing within a few hours after not having touched it for weeks.

My tip: Sepia shells, or cuttlebone, are also used for sharpening the beak, but they should *not* be given to female parakeets *about to breed* because these birds sometimes develop egg binding after gnawing on sepia shells.

Herbs and Wild Plants

Fresh foods can include herbs and wild plants because these resemble the things parakeets eat in the wild.

Your kitchen and garden can supply basil, chervil, and parsley to supplement the bird's diet.

In meadows (unfertilized ones) or along the roadside (but not along roads with automobile traffic) you can gather wild plants when you are out walking.

Scratching the head.

Smoothing the feathers.

Collect half-ripe and ripe seeds from annual grasses and wild millet, the leaves and flowers of bush vetch, tufted vetch, and cow vetch, open seedheads of pansies, flowers and fruits of hawthorn, and leaves and stems of dandelions, chickweed, shepherd's purse, and watercress.

How to offer them: Rinse all herbs and wild plants with lukewarm water, shake dry, and attach bunches of them to the cage roof with a clothespin.

My tip: If you notice your parakeet

In the photos:
Thorough grooming of the plumage is practiced by all birds, for only if the feathers are clean and arranged properly can a bird fly well.

37

A varied diet keeps a parakeet healthy. In addition to a good birdseed mixture the birds need fruit and vegetables. The fresh food should also include herbs and wild greens. Adding multivitamins to the drinking water periodically is recommended.

trying to "bathe" in the moist greenery, quickly offer the bathhouse with water or a shallow dish with a lot of damp greens for a "dew bath" (see page 18).

Things to Enrich the Diet
Available at pet stores

• Spray millet is the most important supplement and is loved best by the birds. A highly nutritious and unadulterated natural food, it is ideal for breeding pairs, nestlings, and young birds, as well as for sick and weak ones.

However, healthy, fully grown birds should not get more than a piece about 2 inches (6 cm) long per day. If they are given more, they will feed almost exclusively on the millet and get too fat. Attach the spray millet to the cage with a clothespin.

• Special seeds, sold in small packages and under names that suggest that they promote easy molting, facilitate learning to talk, and so on, are birdseed mixtures that no doubt are exceptionally high in vitamins and proteins (so far no scientific analysis has been provided) but that a bird receiving

When a parakeet cleans its belly feathers, it draws each one through its beak singly to smooth and oil it.

a good, balanced diet probably doesn't need. I am certain that these special foods have no effect on speaking talent. Learning to talk is something the bird itself has to accomplish, and you have to help it by patiently repeating the phrases to be mastered over and over again (see page 00).

• Hearts, rings, sticks, wheels, and other shapes covered with seeds are sold as parakeet treats. No one knows whether the birds like them because of the taste or simply because they like to gnaw on things. The seeds are glued to the shapes with sugar syrup and honey. Fresh branches are also very healthy and provide "work" for a parakeet's beak.

• On the other hand, giving vitamin supplements seems very sensible to me since it is impossible to check the vitamin content of birdseed—the bird's dietary mainstay—or of fruits and vegetables. Vitamins are crucial to health. The smaller the organism, the more sensitive it is to the lack of vitamins. That is why it is advisable to add vitamins to the bird's drinking water. You can buy multivitamins at drugstores or at the pet store. Look for the expiration date. Vitamins that are too old are useless.

What you can prepare yourself

• Hard-boiled egg yolk mixed with a little low-fat cottage cheese is a valuable protein supplement. About half a teaspoonful a week is beneficial.

• Freshly cracked grain, which you may use in your own breakfast cereal, can also be given to the bird. Soak about a quarter of a teaspoonful a day in a little lukewarm water for your bird.

• Feed your bird sprouted seeds daily for three to four weeks at the following times: in the middle of winter and again in early spring, during the molt, when the female broods, and at times when the bird is not getting much fresh food. This will prevent deficiencies from developing. You can sprout the birdseed you buy at the pet store or whole oat and wheat kernels sold for sprouting at health-food stores. As soon as viable seeds start to absorb water, a chemical reaction is triggered that results in sprouting. In the process, the vitamins, minerals, and trace elments present in the seeds are released and increase, which enhances the nutritional value of soaked and, even more, of sprouted grains and seeds.

Directions for Sprouting Seeds
• Cover 1/2 teaspoonful each of birdseed, whole oat and whole wheat kernels with 3/4 of an inch (2 cm) water and let them soak for 24 hours.
• Rinse the seeds off with lukewarm water, let them drain, then put them in a glass dish and let stand, lightly covered, in the open at room temperature for 48 hours.
• As soon as the sprouts emerge from the seeds, you can offer them to the bird. Rinse them with lukewarm water first and drain well. If you wait another 24 hours, the sprouts will be bigger.

Very important: Don't cover the seeds airtight or they will form mold. Sprouts mold quickly at room temperature. That is why you should throw out any sprouts not consumed within 2 hours.

Snitching at the Table
It is hard to resist the charm of a tame parakeet walking daintily from plate to plate helping itself to a little bit of this and that. But moving around on the table among hot dishes with foods that may be highly spiced or contain other things that don't agree with a bird's digestion is dangerous. The bird can get scalded, burn its tongue, or choke on hot spices. If you decide to let your parakeet join you at the dinner table all the same, you have to watch it constantly and have some foods prepared especially for it, things like a bit of boiled, cooled potato, a little dry white bread, some mildly seasoned vegetable, or some fruit. If the bird is in its cage in the same room when people sit down for a meal, it, too, will begin to eat—from its own dish.

Summary of the Most Important Points
What is healthy for the bird
• Fill a cup with birdseed once a day; remove empty hulls at least twice a day.
• Offer a piece of spray millet about 2 inches (6 cm) long every day.
• Give a bowl of mixed fresh fruits and vegetables twice a day if you can, and provide as much variety as possible.
• Supply a little bunch of fresh herbs or wild greens daily.
• At intervals of four to six weeks treat your parakeet to a period of sprouted seeds.
• Supply fresh drinking water every day, perhaps mixed with a vitamin supplement.
• Make sure the bird always has a mineral block in the cage for sharpening its beak.
What is harmful for the bird
• Cold food fed directly from the refrigerator.
• Rotting or moldy food, even if the bad spots have been removed. Bacteria and fungi continue to grow hidden deep inside the food.
• Salty and spiced food and, of course, plain salt, spices, and sugar.
• Chocolate and other sweets.
• Cream, butter, cheese, and other fats and fatty foods.
• Alcoholic beverages and coffee.
Definitely to be avoided
• Depriving the bird of food, hoping a hungry bird will "eat out of your hand."

A water dispenser keeps the drinking water clean because hardly any dirt can get into the narrow drinking trough.

It's not all that simple . . .   *to gnaw on a spray of millet.*

This is sheer cruelty to animals.

• Small automatic food dispensers. I know from my own experience that these devices stop working when they clog up with dust or empty husks. If the food flow stops entirely, a bird may die of hunger. If you want to use an automatic feeder, make sure the opening and the seed collector at the bottom are large enough and check daily to make sure the food runs through smoothly.

Please keep in mind

Parakeets are members of the parrot family, but their bills are not as strong as those of their larger relatives. They are able to dehusk seeds with their beak and their small, thick tongue, and they can take bites of soft fruit. Harder fruit and root vegetables, like apples and carrots, have to be grated or given in slices lodged firmly enough between the cage bars for the birds to be able to bite off pieces. Parakeets cannot hold onto pieces of food with the foot while eating them the way larger parrots do, and the keeper should therefore do what he or she can to make eating easier. For instance, many parakeets are especially fond of the small seeds on strawberries, but they can only get at them if you hold the berry steady. They also like grapes but can only eat them if they are cut in half. Then, if you hold half a grape up to

The best way is to hold on with one foot . . . and pick out the kernels one by one.

the bird, it may dip into the grape and drink the juice with obvious enjoyment.

Converting Parakeets to Fresh Food

Some parakeets persistently refuse to try fruit, herbs, or vegetables you offer them. They may ignore these healthy additions to their diet for years, until their keeper is utterly discouraged and gives up trying. But sometimes a little ingenuity and the ability to look at the world from the bird's perspective can result in convincing a parakeet of the value of fresh food after all. Thus some friends of mine, who had long tried in vain to give their parakeet fruit and vegetables, finally decided to let the bird join them at breakfast, when there was always plenty of fruit and some health-food bread with whole grains in it. At first the bird only nibbled a little on some dry bread. But when it saw that all the members of its "flock" were eating fruit, its interest was aroused and it wanted to taste some, too. It wasn't long before it got used to eating fruit cut small for it, and from then on it waited with eager anticipation for its breakfast.

I have heard similar stories about other parakeets. One bird would only eat fresh food if its mistress started to eat a piece of fruit it had first spurned.

In the photos:
Spray millet is not only a favorite treat but also a nutritious food. But don't let the bird eat more than about 2 inches worth (6 cm) a day or it will get too fat.

If Your Bird Gets Sick

A Sick Parakeet . . .

. . . usually sits on its favorite perch apathetically, its plumage all puffed up, tail drooping slightly, and avoids all contact. Often the bill is tucked into the back feathers, the eyes are half shut, and the bird rests on both legs, not on one, the way a healthy bird sleeps. With dull eyes it stares into space; it hardly eats anything but drinks all the more. If such a bird is not treated promptly it soon loses so much strength that it can barely balance on the perch any longer and rests almost directly on its abdomen or lies flat on the cage floor. Don't debate too long whether or not to take the bird to the vet, for such a small creature needs help fast.

A bird is not sick if it tries to feed its avian partner, its plastic companion, or its bell or mirror with regurgitated seeds or if it sneezes or yawns occasionally.

How to Help a Sick Bird

Make sure the parakeet's room is very quiet, and provide even warmth. A sick bird needs a cage of its own and should get lukewarm camomile tea to drink. Sometimes the use of an infrared lamp also helps (see page 44).

The Visit to the Veterinarian

If your bird's condition does not improve within a few hours you should take it to an avian veterinarian on the same day or, at the very latest, the next day. If you notice any sign of alarm (see page 43), you have to consult the veterinarian immediately. In many cities, veterinarians can be reached even at night and on holidays in an emergency, but vets very rarely make house calls. Usually you have to take your bird to the doctor.

Please remember

• Replace the sand in the cage bottom with clean paper so that the vet can immediately tell the consistency of the droppings.

• Protect the bird against cold, dampness, and great heat on the way. It is best to put a cover on the cage or carry it in a big box, but make sure that there is sufficient air circulation.

A healthy parakeet produces droppings every 12 to 15 minutes. The drawing shows what these droppings should look like: There should be a dark rim around the white uric acid. Runny droppings can be a sign of illness.

This sick parakeet is squatting apathetically on its perch with half-shut eyes, ruffled feathers, a drooping tail, and in an almost horizontal position.

Health Problems at a Glance

These signs may indicate only a passing indisposition

If accompanied by these symptoms, there is cause for alarm, and treatment by the vet is required.

Apathetic behavior, avoidance of contact.

Staggering, trembling, falling from perch. Possible infection?

Refusing to eat.

Cramping, partial paralysis. Vitamin deficiency? Tumor?

Feeding partner or an object regurgitated seeds; possibly display behavior with a surrogate object.

Tossing pus from the nose, sticky plumage, plugged nares. Crop inflammation?

Breathing difficulties, frequent yawning; may be because of lack of exercise and obesity.

Squeaking and whistling sounds when breathing; bird hangs from cage bar by the beak to breathe easier through stretched trachea. Pneumonia? Thyroid problems?

Frequent sneezing.

Sneezing with runny nasal secretion. Bad cold? Beginning of some other illness?

Mushy to runny droppings for over 1 or 2 hours; food or bath water too cold, change in environment, loneliness, pining.

Droppings are foamy, bloody, or strongly discolored, diarrhea persists. Alarm! Accompanying symptoms of many diseases (kidneys)?

Bird is unable to pass droppings.

Visible straining, cries of pain. Egg binding in female; intestinal blockage?

Limping or dragging one leg or wing; light contusion caused by collision. Lumps under the skin

Leg or wing hangs down limply, no weight is put on one leg. Fracture? Fat deposits, thickening of the preen gland. Tumor? Other growth?

Bleeding from the cloaca or from wounds.

Internal bleeding. Injured blood vessel?

Restless nibbling on the plumage, continual frantic scratching.

Weight loss, dull plumage, feather plucking. Mites or other parasites? Emotional distress?

Spongy brownish growths on bill, cere, and feet.

Tiny mites that spread to other birds. Parakeet mange?

Many feathers fall out; normal molt (see page 46.

Constant molting, bare spots. Mites? Improper diet or hormonal imbalance?

Upper mandible overgrown, toenails too long.

Interferes with eating; toes catch in things. Beak or nails have to be trimmed.

Questions the Vet Will Ask
- How old is the bird?
- When did it first look sick?
- What did you notice particularly?
- Has the bird been sick before?
- Who treated it then and what drugs and other treatments were used?
- What kind of birdseed is the parakeet eating? (Be sure to take along a sample.)
- What does it drink?
- What kinds of fruit and vegetables has it been eating?
- Could it have nibbled on something poisonous?
- What other animals live in your household?

Talking with the Veterinarian
A stool analysis is usually done on the spot or the results are available the next day. If it yields no clear diagnosis, the vet will give the bird shots or other medications based on what he or she thinks is wrong. Be sure to have everything explained to you clearly, especially if biopsies of the skin, mucous membranes, or other tissue are suggested. Discuss in detail whether further treatments make sense, what the chances of success are, how the treatment will affect the bird, and whether there are alternatives. Ask also what would happen if you decided to reject certain treatments.

If Medication Is Required
If you have to give your bird medication, follow the vet's recommendations on dosage, length of therapy, and method of administration conscientiously. Medications in liquid or powdered form are sprinkled or dribbled over the birdseed or added to the drinking water (tablets are crushed). If you do add them to the drinking water, however, you have to make sure the bird doesn't have access to a dripping faucet or can satisfy its thirst by eating juicy fruits and vegetables. If you have

This drawing shows how the toenails should be cut. The blood vessels, which show faintly through the nail, must not be injured.

to make your bird swallow drops, enclose its body loosely in your hand, bend the head slightly backward, and drip the required number of drops next to the tongue.

Treatment with Infrared Light
Set up an infrared bulb of 150 to 250 watts 16 inches (40 cm) away from the cage in such a way that only half of the cage is exposed to its rays. This allows the bird to get out of the heated area if it wants to (see drawing, page 00). Make sure there is enough drinking water available and place a bowl with steaming water near the cage to provide humidity. If necessary, leave the heat lamp on for two days, and turn it on again after a rest of one day. If the patient's health has visibly improved, gradually move the heat lamp farther away from the cage so that the temperature drops very gradually. Make sure, after you turn the infrared lamp off, that the temperature in the room stays even and that there are no drafts.

Important: In cases of partial paralysis—as when the bird is dragging one foot or one wing is drooping—or of cramping, the use of a heat lamp tends to be more harmful than beneficial. In such a case, consult an avian vet as quickly as possible.

Psittacosis
This disease is difficult to diagnose because it shows no clearcut symptoms. Birds that have come down with psittacosis are apathetic, pass droppings that are too soft and often contain traces of blood, have the snuffles, and are short of breath, or the disease may manifest itself in conjunctivitis and slimy secretions at the lower eyelids. All these symptoms can occur singly or in combination. Because of this it is important to watch the bird carefully and to treat it with infrared light when any of these ailments occur and to take the bird to the veterinarian if they persist.

Billing and mutual feeding are activities performed out of love.

In the past psittacosis was greatly feared because humans, too, can be infected with it and because it was sometimes fatal. Imported parrots had to be quarantined because people thought the disease occurred only in these birds. Today we know that native songbirds as well as domestic poultry can get psittacosis, and the disease now usually goes by the name of ornithosis (*ornitho* as in "ornithology") rather than psittacosis (*psittakos* = Greek for "parrot"). In the meantime drugs have been developed that effectively cure the disease in birds as well as in humans if it is treated in good time. If there are any questionable symptoms, the veterinarian can order a laboratory analysis of a fecal sample that will establish whether it is a case of ornithosis or not. Any occurrence of ornithosis has to be reported. Your veterinarian will tell you what has to be done in such a case.

Misshapen Feathers
Feather malformations sometimes occur in older birds. Flight feathers, tail feathers, and contour feathers remain

45

E ven if your parakeet hasn't shown any sign of illness yet, you should ask your pet dealer or other bird owners for the name of a veterinarian who has experience in the treatment of pet birds.

stuck in their sheaths with only a small brushlike tuft flaring out at the top. Sometimes feathers taper halfway up and then twist around their own axis. Nutritional deficiencies, hormone imbalances, poor blood supply, or cysts in the feather follicle can cause abnormal feathers, which should be treated by the veterinarian.

Feather Plucking

This "bad habit" is not widespread among parakeets. It is usually the larger parrots that succumb to it. Still, feather plucking does occur in parakeets. The affected birds keep plucking feathers until bald and bloody spots appear. Many ornithologists ascribe this compulsive behavior to psychological causes, while others think that the birds accidentally discover the fluid inside the quills when preening and become addicted to it. Whatever the explanation, there is unfortunately no effective way to break a bird of this habit. The situation is most promising if the bird started plucking its plumage in reaction to a psychologically

When using an infrared lamp, cover half the cage with a cloth, so that the bird can get away from the lamp's rays if it gets too hot.

stressful situation, as when the usual caretaker has been away but can now again devote plenty of time to the bird. Usually, however, the cause is not this simple, especially in parakeets, in whom feather plucking is almost always a sign of some health problem. In these birds, feather plucking is almost always associated with nutritional deficiencies, abnormal metabolism, or parasites. A parakeet that plucks its feathers should therefore be taken to an avian veterinarian with experience in this area.

The Molt

The molt is not a disease, but for somewhat older parakeets it is a period of increased physical strain on the organism, during which the birds should get especially nutritious food and be kept evenly warm in a quiet environment. During the molt birds replace their plumage. Many feathers are lost and replaced with new ones within a few days or weeks. During this time the bird peck and nibble on their plumage more than usual and in a way that is clearly different from the usual preening. If the molt is particularly abrupt, the bird may temporarily be unable to fly and will then need your help. I used to stretch hefty strings in strategic places during these times, so that the grounded bird could get from the floor to the cage and from the cage to the bird tree.

French Molt

In the French molt, which is a disorder that affects parakeets, the feathers never develop completely. Nestlings can develop French molt. They are then usually unable to fly but do become tame. Such birds should never be housed together with healthy, breeding birds because the latter can become infected and may produce young with French molt.

If You Want To Have Baby Birds

Is It a True Pair?

If you want your birds to produce offspring you first have to make sure you have a true pair — that is, a male and a female or hen.

Sure sign of a male

If the cere above the bill is blue, this is a sure sign. If your bird is a lutino, albino, fallow, or a recessive pied (birds with splotches of color, also called harlequins), the cere will be pink.

Sure sign of a female

All female parakeets have buff colored to light brown ceres.

Are They Compatible?

If your two birds touch bills and preen each other, you will sooner or later see them get ready to mate. But it takes a while, for love at first sight is rare with parakeets.

It's quite possible that your two parakeets will get along famously without developing any sexual interest in each other. This is not surprising since they never had a chance to really choose their mate, a process which, in wild parakeets, is a crucial step toward forming a lifelong pair bond. If your pair shows no interest in courtship, mating, and brooding, you can add another male. Perhaps this second male will stir the reproductive instinct in the female.

It would be a mistake to add a second female to the pair. Females compete for a single male and fight viciously if they cannot get out of each other's sight.

Declaration of Love and Courtship Displays

The male, which at the start acts rather cautiously toward the female, visibly gains self-confidence. More and more often he moves right next to her and eagerly taps his bill against hers. She in turn hacks at him less and less frequently to keep him at a distance. On the contrary, she now begins to approach him in a slightly bent over

The posture of a parakeet female ready to mate is almost coquettish. For a few seconds she stands still with her head thrown back and the tail raised high.

posture and lets him feed her. In his growing sexual excitement the male tries to step on the female's tail, to which she responds by whirling around instantly and protesting vociferously. But she seems to understand his intent, for there is never any active show of aggression.

The male now tries to impress his mate. He pulls on the bell in the cage with all his might, making it swing madly around his head, circles around the

47

The eyes are open.

The wing feathers are growing in.

gesture. She raises her tail straight up and throws her head back. Then she remains motionless in this graceful pose. The male, in apparent confusion, alternates between putting one foot on her back and touching bills with her until he has gathered the courage to mount her. Holding on to the neck feathers of the female, he folds one or both wings around her and presses his cloaca against hers so that his semen can get to her oviduct.

The Nest Box

To help your birds get into a reproductive mood, place a nest box in the cage or in the bird tree. You can buy commercial nest boxes measuring 10 x 6 x 6 inches (25 x 15 x 15 cm). In the wall of the longer side there is an entrance hole with a perch below it. Inside the box there is a block with a hollow in it. The top of the box flips open for easy checking of the nest and the nestlings.

Life Changes

At first the birds respond to the nest with irritation and avoid it. But the female has some idea of what it is for. She eventually approaches it hesitantly and peeks through the entrance hole. Soon she gets brave enough to slip in for a moment. Then she starts working inside the box, chipping at the hollow in the block to make it a little deeper. She stays inside the box a bit longer every day, letting the male feed her but normally refusing to let him in. If a male parakeet persists and penetrates into the box anyway, this is a phenomenon due to domestication; in the wild the female would never permit it.

The First Egg

The female deposits the first egg about eight days after the mating. Before laying the first egg, young females sometimes make themselves sleek and slender and spread their

room in rapid flight, approaches again to give her a gentle nudge with the bill, then runs up and down in front of her excitedly, nodding and bowing continually. He keeps talking the whole time, makes the feathers on his throat and forehead stand on end, and his eyes take on their typical courtship look with the pupils contracting into tiny dots. The female doesn't seem to be overly impressed by all his eager devotion, but at some point she will indicate her readiness to mate in a charming

In the photos:
A parakeet chick, which weighs only 2 grams when it emerges from its shell, grows into an independent creature within 5 weeks. After its prenuptial molt at 3 to 4 months of age, the bird is sexually mature.

ll the downy feathers are already present.

wings, trembling. The droppings at this me get runnier and are passed in reater amounts. The cere above the bill ecomes lighter in color and smoother han before. If the first egg drops to the oor because the nest box wasn't ready, he female has a hard time maintainig er balance on the perch. Shaking, she ans out the feathers on her wings, vhich are raised high, and bites into the mpty air. After a few minutes she ecovers. If there is no nest box, no urther attention is paid to the egg, or it may be destroyed.

Time to Brood

If the female has deposited her first egg inside the nest box, she hardly emerges from the box anymore because she starts to sit on the egg right away. She keeps on laying an egg every other day until there is a clutch of three to five eggs, rarely more. The baby birds will later hatch in the same order and at the same invervals as the eggs were laid. The egg of a parakeet weighs 2 grams,

49

exactly the same as a newly hatched chick. The mother bird now leaves her box only three or four times a day to defecate. She is fed exclusively by the male and sticks her head out of the entrance hole only to get food. Even though the male stays close by, keeping guard and reassuring his mate with songs and short calls, the female checks the situation with quick glances at the slightest unaccustomed sound.

Important for Successful Brooding

• The female wants to hear her mate near the nest box. Commotion, noise, and other disturbing activities in the room can bother her enough to make her stop laying or brooding, especially during the first few days.

• Once the female has settled down on the eggs she is less easily upset, and you can occasionally lift the cover and peer into the nest box without ill effects.

• After about 10 days you can take advantage of the female's brief periods of absence to check the eggs. Hold each egg up to a light; fertilized eggs are bluish and slightly opaque. They look darker than infertile ones, which are light and translucent.

• Remove infertile eggs only if there are more than four eggs in the clutch. Too great a change might irritate the female and make her cease brooding.

• For healthy development of the embryos, a steady temperature of about 72° F (22° C), fresh air, and a humidity level of 60% are important. To achieve the right humidity, you can set up a humidifier, or you can simply place a large bowl of water, covered by a wire screen, in the room.

• If there are droppings on the eggs, don't try to wipe or wash them off because this could be harmful to the embryonic chicks. A waxlike layer on the shell protects the eggs against infections.

• Once the baby birds have hatched you should check the nest daily. A chick occasionally dies, and the decomposition of the body, which sets in quickly, would endanger the other nestlings.

There will be more on the brooding and development of baby parakeets in the next chapter.

Understanding Parakeets

Why Does It Do What It Does?

Since the publication of our first pet-owner's manual on parakeets I have received several hundred letters from parakeet owners asking all kinds of questions. Many of the letters were from children who wanted to know what various striking ways of moving, repeated patterns of behavior, calls, or other habits of their bird meant. In most cases I had to answer that no two parakeets are exactly alike and that each bird has its own peculiarities. But there are some types of behavior that are common to all parakeets, such as the melodic whistling or the quiet whetting of the bill that is observed in a relaxed and happy parakeet. Not every sequence of movements is necessarily associated with a specific mood; rather, moods tend to be expressed through certain motions and calls common to the species.

Typical Movements

Stretching of the legs: Ever so often a parakeet will stretch one leg and at the same time extend the wing of the same side. This gesture is comparable to the stretching we do when we get tired of sitting or standing in the same position. When the leg is pulled up again, the toes are often curled into a fist. If you notice that your parakeet is always stretching the same leg or isn't executing the gesture at all, this might be the first sign of some abnormal weakness. Watch the bird carefully, and take it to the veterinarian if necessary.

Resting on one leg: The stretching of the leg often ends with the leg being retracted into the ventral feathers. Of course, the pulling up of the leg is not always preceded by stretching. Para-keets also usually have one leg tucked close to the body in their sleeping stance, although many parakeets sleep standing on both legs. So you have to know your bird and its habits well to be able to tell if such small deviations from the norm are just peculiarities typical of your bird or an indication that something isn't quite right. One thing you can safely assume is that if your bird is resting on one leg it feels relaxed and is well.

Bill tucked into the back feathers: Parakeets are very limber and can turn

After laying an egg, a parakeet female retains her balance only with great effort. A sick bird suffering pain can look the same way.

their heads 180 degrees. They do this whenever they bury their bill in their slightly ruffled shoulder feathers. Most parakeets sleep in this posture, though they also assume it during the day in

Quite often parakeets grind their bill softly before tucking it into the back feathers and going to sleep. This is a sign of utter comfort and contentment.

f a parakeet is leaping around in its cage performing all kinds of daring twists and turns, this usually means that it would like to be let out to fly. Often it reinforces this request with loud shrieking.

periods of inactivity. Sometimes they chirp very softly at the same time.

Raising of the wings: Perhaps more often than they stretch their legs, parakeets raise their folded wings. This, too, is a relaxing kind of stretching, but birds also assume this posture when they are getting a little overheated. It allows them to give off some body heat. Often, however, raising the wings is simply a gesture of contentment or relief.

Extending the wings sideways: The wings are spread sideways if a bird wants to impress its mate or a rival. However, if it flattens its plumage, making itself appear extremely sleek and slim and, in addition, bites at the empty air, this is a sign of extreme pain or terror.

Typical Activities

Preening the head: A parakeet cannot groom its head with its bill. If there is no companion to perform this labor of love, the parakeet has to resort to its toes for scratching and cleaning the head. To do this it cannot raise its foot directly to the head, passing it in front of the wing, but insetad sticks it around in back of the wing, which looks awkward and comical. Ornithologists regard the way birds raise their legs—either in front of or behind the wing—with considerable interest because the particular method used gives some clues about the evolutionary relationship between different kinds of birds.

A parakeet also grooms its head by rubbing it against the cage bars or a perch.

Flapping the wings: Young birds in particular flap their wings vigorously while holding on tight to the perch they are sitting on. This is a way of exercising the wing muscles, which still need strengthening. Adult parakeets also flap their wings if they haven't had a chance to fly for some time. Another time for wing flapping is at the end of the molt,

when the loss of too many feathers all at once may have rendered the bird flightless and it cannot satisfy its urge for aerial exercise. Birds that flap their wings should be allowed to fly as soon as possible unless you know for sure that they are unable to for some reason.

Yawning: All birds, including parakeets, yawn, opening their bills extremely wide. If your bird yawns all the time, you should air the room thoroughly. Being creatures of the air, birds are much more sensitive to stale air than humans. By the way, yawning is just as contagious in birds as it is in people. If one begins to yawn, its partner or the whole flock in a flight will soon be yawning too. This contagiousness of mood is typical for parakeets. If one bird starts to preen itself, its neighbors will soon follow suit, and the same pattern dominates broodiness, sleeping, and eating.

Sneezing: Sometimes birds produce sounds that are very similar to our sneezing. However, avian sneezing is not caused by the same things as human sneezing; birds sneeze to clear their nasal passages.

Shaking the feathers: Parakeets always terminate a preening session with a good shake of the entire fluffed up plumage. This makes sense, for the bill has dislodged minute dust particles that are sent flying to the floor by the shaking. But sometimes you will see a similar shaking motion when the bird hasn't been grooming itself at all. Birds always shake themselves before they engage in a new activity. If your parakeet has been resting, for instance, and decides to go and have a drink, it usually shakes itself first. Shaking also relieves tension. If a parakeet has been

A pair of parakeets mating. The excitement makes the pupils contract so that they show up only as black dots in the middle of the white iris.

uneasy or alarmed for some reason, it will shake itself as soon as the tension lets up.

Whetting the bill: After every meal, and sometimes in between as well, a parakeet rubs its bill against its perch. In part this practice serves to clean the bill and keep the mandibles in proper shape. That is why it is important that natural branches be available to be used this way.

Consciousness of tail: Their tails seem to be particularly important to parakeets. The tail is cleaned, oiled, and smoothed more often than any other part of the body, and this grooming chore is never entrusted to a partner. Apparently parakeets have a special sensory capacity that tells them whether their tail is being touched by some object—which is accepted as unavoidable—or by a living creature, which must be fought at all cost. It is an important point for anyone trying to win the bird's trust and not to lose it. If you have a pair of birds, you will also see that the tail

After sleeping or sitting still for some time, a parakeet needs to stretch. It does this by extending one leg, along with the wing of the same side, backward.

plays a role in the courtship display. When the male approaches the female with the intention of mating, he trips along the floor trying repeatedly to step on her tail. She resists by dodging him cleverly but doesn't respond aggressively.

Alarm calls and shrieking: It is well known that parakeets sometimes shriek for prolonged periods. Up to now there has been no plausible explanation for these agitated vocalizations, which wild parakeets apparently don't produce since no one has mentioned observing this behavior in them. I myself have owned parakeets for over 12 years but have never heard them shrieking, although I wished I would. I have, however, heard them emit shrill alarm calls quite often, combined with abrupt departure from the branch they were perching on, even when there was no sign of a raptor outside the window. This shows that parakeets, even when they have been bred in captivity for many generations, have not "forgotten" their original natural behavior.

Typical Capabilities

Vision: Like all birds that are active during the day, parakeets see the world in colors. This is to be expected since the colorful plumage of many birds serves definite functions in their social interaction. Birds also have almost panoramic vision because their eyes are located on the sides of the head, enabling them to spot enemies over a wide range and take cover. The area taken in simultaneously by both eyes is smaller than in humans, but parakeets can absorb 150 images per second. By comparison, the human eye absorbs only 16. For fast-flying birds quick detection of details is crucial to survival.

Hearing: It is not surprising that birds have an acute sense of hearing when you consider that they have to be able to communicate over large distances with calls and songs. Their hearing also has to be highly differentiated—that is, the birds have to be able to distinguish small differences in sound frequencies to be able to interpret all the different vocal expressions and respond appropriately. What sounds like uniform shrieking to the human ear is recognizable to a parakeet as a specific sequence of notes. This sequence of notes is recognized by a partner and can even be repeated "verbatim."

Taste: No studies have been done on the gustatory capacities of parakeets.

If a parakeet wants to scratch its head, it raises a foot up behind the wing.

But anyone who has watched one of these birds sample food at the family table knows that it goes after some things eagerly and pays no attention to others. I am convinced that parakeets have nerve endings that are highly sensitive to taste.

Smell: I myself have very little sense of how well parakeets can smell. But a parakeet expert of my acquaintance is convinced that parakeets can smell just as well as we can.

Sense of touch: It is beyond question that birds surpass humans in this area. Their tactile capacities are highly developed as shown, for instance, by the fact that a brooding parakeet female is able to sense the chick's movements within the shell with her brood patch (a small, almost bare area on the breast with good blood circulation) and thus know when the

chick is about to hatch. Birds also have a special sensitivity to vibrations, which makes them detect the slightest tremors. Birds even interpret the sources of such tremors correctly and thus have early warning of approaching enemies and natural events. Because of this sensitivity to vibration the cage of a parakeet should be in a place that is absolutely stable.

My tip: The vibration of the refrigerator motor can frighten a parakeet half to death. Never put the cage near the refrigerator, even for a short moment.

Embarrassment: A parakeet that is all set to fly spontaneously up to a trusted human may, if at the last moment it notices something new and visually striking in the person, stop bewildered and begin to preen itself instead of taking to the air. This is a bird's way of expressing embarrassment. My parakeet Manky used to enjoy playing with marbles on my desk. He would run after them or toward them, ready to give them a kick. But if two marbles rolled toward him simultaneously from the side instead of from straight ahead, this seemed somehow ominous to him, and he would immediately run to his food dish and start eating.

What Are All These Skills for?
When you read in the next few pages how parakeets live and survive in their Australian homeland, you will gain a better understanding of why nature has equippped these birds with so many skills and abilities.

Description of a Parakeet
Parakeets are part of the Psittacinae, the seventh subfamily of the parrot family. They are the only species of their genus, which is included in the tribe Platycercini (rosellas and allies), and there are no subspecies.
Scientific name: *Melopsittacus undulatus.* The first of these Latin

I f a parakeet feels embarrassed it often begins to preen itself busily or picks nervously at the band on its foot. Ethologists use the term "displacement activity" for this kind of behavior.

In the photo:
In nature, parakeets communicate with each other with certain calls, thus maintaining vocal contact with each other. Shrill, short alarm calls are warnings that a predator is near.

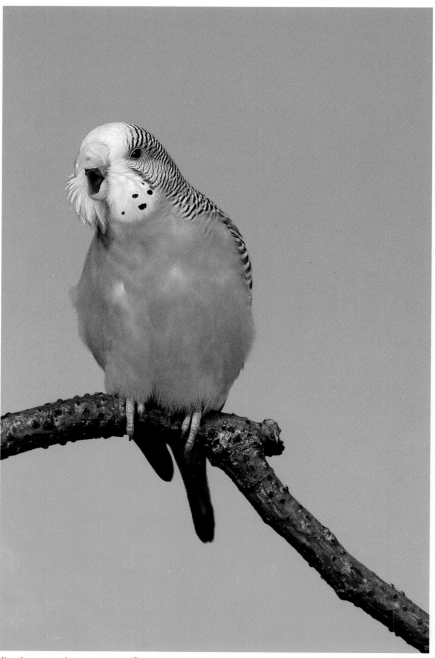

I'm here—where are you?

names comes from the Greek and means "singing parrot." "Undulatus" comes from the Latin word "unda," wave, and refers to the birds' undulating markings. In English, the birds are also known as "budgies," short for budgerigar, or as shell parakeets.

Origin: Australia.

Habitat: Shrubby grasslands in Central Australia, especially along shallow streams with intermittent water flow (called "creeks" in Australia).

Original wild form: Green with a yellow mask and wavy black-and-yellow markings on the back of the head, the upper back, and the wings.

Overall length without tail: 6 1/4 to 7 inches (16–18 cm)

Tail: 3 to 3 1/2 inches (8–9 cm)

Weight: 1 to 1.4 ounces (30–40 g)

Life expectancy: 12 to 14 years

Sexual maturity: At 3 to 4 months of age

Size of clutch: 3 to 5 eggs

Egg laying: At intervals of 2 days

Beginning of incubation: After the first egg

Length of incubation: 18 days

Nestling period: 28 to 32 days

The Hard Nomadic Life

Living conditions in the hot, arid climate of Central Australia are extremely harsh. Sometimes it doesn't rain for months or even years at a time. The temperature in the morning and evening is 100° F (38° C) and climbs to 113° F (45° C) and higher during the day. Parakeets therefore spend the midday hours sitting in groups of 50 or so birds high up in the eucalyptus trees that grow along the creeks. They stay in the trees quietly and unobtrusively and, with their cryptic coloring, are practically invisible. This quiet way of life during the dry season is also due in part to the need to conserve water. The less active a creature is, the less water it uses up. The parakeets forage on the ground for food early in the morning and toward evening. At night the temperature drops very rapidly; after midnight it can go below freezing. These cool and sometimes downright cold nights luckily produce dew, which the birds absorb off the grass in the morning and which they fall back on for drinking water during dry periods. However, if there is water in the streams or in rock declivities, parakeets drink about every three hours. Some other parrots only drink in the morning and evening. If there is no rain for long periods, the grasses and other plants dry up, and the few seeds are soon eaten up. Then the parakeets are forced by the scarcity of food to set off in search of new pastures.

Since deserts and semideserts in Australia extend over hundreds and thousands of miles, the birds often have to fly several hundred miles before they find an area that offers enough food. The birds set off on their long flights not only in small groups but also in huge flocks. If a flock travels over a long distance like this, all the birds fly very fast and keep in contact with each other with certain kinds of calls.

Misconceptions

One misconception of the needs of parakeets is demonstrated by owners and breeders who keep their birds in an outdoor aviaries all year round without providing a heated shelter. These people argue that parakeets are used to severe weather since they survive cold nights in their native areas. It is true that parakeets do survive below-freezing weather in our temperate zones, but Mr. H. J. Michaelis, who knows a great deal about parakeets, has expressed the situation aptly: Parakeets do survive cold winters in outdoor aviaries, but they aren't really living; they merely vegetate. After all, in Australia the temperature drops below freezing only for a few hours at a time during the night, not for weeks on end.

The modest need for water of

When on their way to nearby feeding grounds or watering places, wild parakeets cover short distances by swooping over the tree tops in an undulating pattern. When covering long distances, the flocks fly straight as an arrow and very fast.

Pair bonds among parakeets last for life, until one of the partners dies. It is the female who determines whether or not such a bond will be formed.

parakeets gives rise to another misunderstanding. Under normal circumstances parakeets drink more frequently than other members of the parrot family, but they drink much less at a time. Experiments have shown that parakeets can survive without water for up to 28 days at a temperature of 86° F (30° C) and a humidity of only 30%. Dr. Karl Immelmann comments: "In spite of the ability to do without water for considerable periods of time—which no doubt represents an adaptation to 'emergency' conditions—parakeets stay close to water if they can."

It is incorrect, therefore, to maintain that parakeets are perfectly comfortable in extended periods of below-freezing temperatures and that they don't need anything to drink.

What is correct is that parakeets are

When in a fighting mood, male parakeets threaten each other with open beaks and use their feet to kick the opponent in the chest.

comfortable when it is warm. They become inactive only when it is very hot, and thanks to their plumage they can resist the cold of freezing weather for short periods. They are most alive and active in temperatures around 68° F (20° C). It is also true that parakeets like to take frequent small drinks of water and that they enjoy baths.

When It Rains It's Time to Breed

When, in the course of their wanderings, parakeets come to an area where it has recently rained or where rain is still falling, their whole way of life changes. Rain brings moisture and cooler weather. It makes plants grow green again; there will soon be abundant supplies of half-ripe seeds, which are indispensible for raising baby parakeets. The males immediately start going through their courtship rituals to put the females into a broody mood, and the females get busy looking for suitable nesting cavities. Holes high up in eucalyptus trees are ideal. The female enlarges the inside of the cavity with her beak, makes sure there is a bowl-like hollow in the bottom, and works on the entrance hole. The fine chips produced by her beak work serve as padding for the eggs and later for the nestlings.

Since small contingents of the large flying flock always stick together, groups of a few closely spaced trees become hives of avian activity. Several breeding pairs usually nest in the same tree. The courtship activity of the male and the busy work of the female are contagious. Within a few days the tree holes are occupied, matings take place, and the first eggs are about to be laid in the protective cavities. No one hardly ever catches sight of a female; they brood the eggs steadily, emerging from their holes only to relieve themselves. While they sit on the eggs the females are fed by the males. They get off the clutch only briefly and stick their heads out of the entry hole to receive food. In the wild, the male is not allowed into the nest cavity.

Incubation

The female lays an egg every other

day, and incubation begins as soon as the first egg is laid. At regular intervals the eggs are turned and the ones on the outside are rolled to the center of the nest. When a chick is ready to hatch after 18 days, it has already communicated that fact to its mother with soft peepings from inside the shell. It has also set to work on the inside of the shell with its "egg tooth," a thorn-shaped projection on the bill. It takes the chick 20 hours of chipping while rotating continually and and pushing until it is free of its shell. Sometimes the mother helps by breaking off small bits of the shell.

The chicks hatch in the same order the eggs were laid. Naked and blind, they immediately disappear under the mother's plumage and are fed by her. When several chicks have hatched, the oldest one is always first in line for feeding and receives food from the mother's crop while the youngest initially gets predigested food from the mother's glandular stomach (proventriculus).

Life in a Flock

After the young leave the nesting cavity the father still looks after them for about two weeks. After that they are fully independent and live together with the juvenile birds of the entire flock, while the parents, if there is a sufficient food supply, are busy with their next brood.

First attempts at courtship: Even before the young birds, which have only recently left their parents, undergo their first molt they begin to engage in courtship displays. At first it is only the males; they woo not only females their own age but also, and preferably, ones that are already busy working on a nesting cavity. By contrast, young females tend to favor older males.

If a female doesn't like the courting male, she makes aggressive hacking motions toward him when he approaches, but if he meets her fancy she

Development of the Young at a Glance

1st to 5th day: The chick's eyes are still shut and it is fed while lying on its back.

6th day: The eyes begin to open.

7th day: The primaries start to grow in.

8th day: The chick can hold up its head and take its first steps.

9th day: The tail feathers begin to grow in.

12th day: All the down feathers have grown in.

17th day: The young reaches adult weight of 1 ounce (30 g).

28th day: The flight and tail feathers have almost reached their full length. The young bird can fly and leaves the nest.

38th day: The plumage is fully formed, but the coloration is somewhat duller than that of the parents.

3rd to 4th month: Prenuptial molt. The new plumage is similar to that of adult parakeets, and the birds are sexually mature.

bills and coos with him and soon lets him feed her and scratch her head.

Marriage for life: Once a bond has been formed between a pair of parakeets, it usually lasts for life, as it does in most parrot species. This makes especially good sense for parakeets because the birds don't have to waste time choosing mates this way. When a flock finds itself in an area where conditions for breeding are good, even the youngest members can settle down to the breeding business without first having to find partners. They are already paired and can go about their mating displays, the search for nest sites, and reproduction without delay.

Molting in a hurry: The only time

When a flock gets ready to search for new feeding grounds after breeding, the young are able, even before the prenuptial molt, to undertake the long flight.

59

A parakeet
female
defends her
clutch and
nestlings very
energetically
against other
kinds of birds that
may want to take
over the nesting
cavity.

parakeets are sure to stay in the same place for a while is when they breed. That is why they also use this time to partially replace their plumage in a so-called "soft molt." Then, when they have to set out on long journeys again, their plumage is intact and ready.

Enemies are everywhere: Parakeets are always aware of what is going on above them because originally attack from higher flying raptors was their main threat. They don't have an innate warning system oriented to enemies on the ground and are therefore easy prey to cats that have been introduced into Australia. Other birds competing for nesting cavities represent another danger. Although female parakeets defend their cavities and their eggs or young with great courage against intruders, they don't always prevail.

How do they communicate with each other? Parakeets are considered the quietest of the Australian parrots. Their vocal repertoire is less varied than that of many of our native songbirds. We have already mentioned that during the dry season parakeets keep so quiet that many observers become aware of their presence only by accident. During the resting periods their cryptic green coloring lets them completely fade into the foliage of the eucalyptus trees on which they perch. Since they feel safest when high up in the air, they congregate near the tops of the trees. From there, their soft twitterings hardly reach the ears of birdwatchers. When the birds forage on the the ground, they usually remain quiet, too. Only occasionally a louder call is heard. This call, which serves to maintain contact within the flock, always sounds the same to our human ears. But parakeets not only understand the message of the call, "We are here, where are you?" but can also tell by fine nuances of sound which individual bird it comes from.

Nuances of communication are even more important when the active,

reproductive phase of life starts. Now it is a matter of maintaining a minimum distance between birds, so that the communal life of the flock can go on without the interference of aggressive acts, while at the same time respecting the privacy of the individual pairs.

Bibliography and Addresses

Books

Binks, Gerald S. *Best in Show, Breeding and Exhibiting Budgerigars*. Elburry Press, London.

Stan and Barbara Moizer. *The Complete Budgerigars*. Barron's, Hauppauge, New York.

Vriends, Matthew M. *The New Bird Handbook*. Barron's, Hauppauge, New York.

Magazines

American Cage Bird Magazine
One Glamore Court
Smithtown, NY 11787

Bird Talk
P.O. Box 3940
San Clemente, CA 92672

The AFA Watchbird
2208 "A" Artesia Boulevard
Redondo Beach, CA 90278

Cage & Aviary Birds
Prospect House,
9-15 Ewell Road
Cheam, Sutton, Surrey, SM3 8B2
England

Organizations

American Budgerigar Society
Home Office: 141 Hill Street ext.
Naugatuck, CT 06770

The Budgerigar Society (England)
57, Stephyn's Chambers,
Bank Cour
Marlowes, Hemel Hempstead, Herts

The Avicultural Society of Queensland
c/o Mr. Ray Garwood
19 Fahey's Road
Albany Creek, 4035, Queensland
Australia

The Golden Triangle Parrot Club
P.O. Box 1574, Station C
Kitchener, Ontario
Canada N2G 4P2

Index

Bold face indicates color photos